Doris Stokes is a celebrated clairaudient who has confounded
sceptics by the uncanny accuracy of her readings. In
Australia she filled Sydney Opera House and was mobbed in
the streets. In America, 'Charlie's Angels' was removed from
a prime television slot to make way for her. In this country
her appearances on radio phone-ins have caused an avalanche
of mail. In her first book, VOICES IN MY EAR, Doris told
how she discovered in herself this extraordinary gift and how
she has shared it with the world. Now, in MORE VOICES
IN MY EAR, she continues her amazing story.

Also by Doris Stokes with Linda Dearsley

VOICES IN MY EAR, THE AUTOBIOGRAPHY OF A MEDIUM

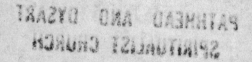

Doris Stokes
with Linda Dearsley

More Voices in My Ear

Futura
Macdonald & Co
London & Sydney

A Futura Book

First published in Great Britain in 1981
by Macdonald Futura Publishers Limited
Reprinted 1981 (three times), 1982

ISBN 0 7088 2100 6

Filmset, printed and bound in Great Britain by
Hazell Watson & Viney Ltd, Aylesbury, Bucks

Futura Publications
A Division of
Macdonald & Co (Publishers) Ltd
Maxwell House
Worship Street
London EC2A 2EN

CHAPTER 1

It was a stormy night. The rain had stopped, but a wind had sprung up and it was getting stronger every minute. Everything was in motion. Tattered clouds were flying across the moon, great black branches tossed against the sky, dead leaves whirled along the gutter and the six of we WRAFs, brave because we were in a group, decided to take the short cut home through the churchyard.

We joked nervously as we approached the path. Beneath wildly plunging trees the silent gravestones stood in rows, now in moonlight, now in shadow. Wet twigs slapped against our hair, strange dark shapes bobbed by the fence and our skirts tangled round our legs making it difficult to walk. The six of us huddled closer together, yet each voice grew a little louder, a little more daring.

'Bet you wouldn't walk across one of those graves!'

'I would too.'

'The spooks'd get you.'

'Spooks!' Molly's voice rose in derision. 'Don't tell me you believe in spooks.'

'Bet you wouldn't stay here all night.'

'No. I've got more sense. I'd freeze to death.'

I listened to them and laughed. You wouldn't have got me staying there all night either and not because of the cold. I wasn't going to let on but the place gave me the creeps. All those gloomy tomb stones. They made me shudder. I glanced across at the church, a pretty stone building in daylight, but now just a black hulk against the sky, and as the moon came out again I stopped in surprise. There were people standing outside the church door. A whole family by the look of it; a man, a woman and two children, just standing there, patiently waiting. What in

5

the world could they be doing? Surely the vicar hadn't arranged to meet them at this time of night.

'I wonder what those people are doing on a night like this,' I said to the other girls.

'What people?' asked Molly.

'Those people over there.'

They looked vaguely up and down the path. 'Where?'

'Over there,' I said pointing impatiently. 'Look, standing by the church door. A whole family.'

They peered in the direction I indicated, and then looked back at me. There was an odd pause and then suddenly, without a word being spoken, they all turned round and ran. Bewildered, I stared after them. What had I said? I glanced back at the family, still waiting, their clothes strangely unruffled in the gale. And then my heart lurched violently. Before my eyes they disappeared. They didn't walk away, they just went out like flames in the wind. For perhaps two seconds I just stood there, my mouth open, staring at the empty space and then I hitched up my skirt and ran as fast as my sensible shoes would allow me.

That was in 1943 and looking back now it seems very funny to think that I ran away from spirit people. I'd had quite a job persuading the girls afterwards that I'd made the whole thing up. After all they'd seen my white, terrified face as I hurtled out of the graveyard behind them, and even though I had a reputation for being a bit of a clown they couldn't help feeling I'd been able to see something that they couldn't. They looked at me a little strangely after that. It was my childhood all over again. Mother always feared I'd end up mad or, at the very least, a bit peculiar and scolded me if I saw or heard anything that other people couldn't. Sometimes I'd come home from school and tell her that one of our acquaintances had died.

'What were you doing round there when you're supposed to come straight home?' Mum used to demand.

'I did come straight home,' I'd protest.

'Then how d'you know Mrs So and So's gone?'

I'd look at the floor and shuffle uncomfortably. 'I – I just know, that's all,' I'd mumble. I really had no idea how I knew, I just *did* know. So I'd get a clout for failing to come straight home from school and a clout for telling lies, on the grounds that I must be guilty of one or the other, or more likely both.

There was no way of knowing then that I was a natural medium. I didn't even know what a medium was and I hated my 'funny streak'. I wanted to be the same as everyone else. It's only as I've grown older and as my powers have developed that I've come to realize what a wonderful gift I've been given.

Since my last book *Voices in My Ear* was published, I've been overwhelmed by letters from all over the world. I feel quite sorry for the postman who has to struggle up to our second floor flat with such great sacks of mail. Unfortunately it's impossible for me to reply to everyone – I'd be busy from morning till night and wouldn't have time for my work – but I try to read them all and they are very moving. One man working in Germany wrote to tell me that he'd sent for the book after hearing me on the radio. Shortly afterwards he and his wife lost their baby daughter. 'That book,' he said, 'gave us strength to go through what we had to face.'

Another woman wrote to say she had never had any experience of mediums but one day she was in a shop and she turned round and saw a smiling face looking at her from the cover of a book. She picked it up, read the blurb on the back and thought, 'Oh, I don't know. I don't go in for this sort of thing.' But she bought it anyway, took it home and read it from cover to cover in one sitting. It opened a whole new set of ideas for her, she says. The idea that death isn't to be feared, that it's a great adventure to look forward to; the idea that we don't go anywhere alone

7

and when our time comes, somebody will take us by the hand and lead us.

It's strange to think that this ability that used to frighten me so much should have enabled me to help so many thousands of people, even people I've never met. And, I'm very glad to say, people don't run away from me any more. These days they flock to my door and I have more invitations to visit overseas than I can cope with.

In the spring of 1979 my husband John and I were invited back to New York. We'd been there briefly the year before but this time we were able to get a much stronger impression. On the first morning we left our hotel with our friends Mike and Bill who were looking after us. It was a cool, blustery day, and I looked up at the sky to see if it might rain. My head went back and back as my eyes scanned acres of concrete and glass until, way up above, I could see a thin strip of grey. It was like being at the foot of monstrous great cliffs and the sensation made me feel quite dizzy. Quickly I dragged my eyes back to the ground and then stopped dead in horror. I'd nearly tripped over the body of a man sprawled across the pavement. Clothes awry, one arm flung out beside him, the man was quite motionless.

'Mike, quick we must do something!' I cried, dropping to my knees. 'This man's ill.' But to my surprise Mike hauled me up again and steered me round the body.

'Leave him, Doris,' he said firmly. 'It's drink or drugs. He'll sleep it off. You'll see a lot like him in New York.'

I looked anxiously over my shoulder. No-one else seemed the least bit worried. Pedestrians were stepping over the body as calmly as if it was a pile of litter. John and I exchanged glances. It wasn't like this in Fulham.

There was worse to come. A little further on we came to a doorway where a pathetic creature, hardly recognizable as a woman, sat huddled in newspapers, two or three grubby bags pressed close to her side.

Bill saw me look at her. 'She's a bag lady, Doris.'

'A what?'

'A bag lady,' he repeated and went on to explain that the bag people, men and women, lived rough, endlessly wandering the city streets carrying their belongings in bags. It seemed terribly sad. I know people sleep rough on the Embankment in London, but here they were in the main streets of the city. It was a shock to see these poor bag people in their newspapers lying outside the luxurious shops of New York's famous avenues.

The pace of life was extraordinary. Leaving early one morning John nudged me. 'Look at that!' he said grinning and my mouth fell open in amazement at the sight of a businessman, briefcase tucked under his arm, a cup of coffee in one hand and a hot dog in the other, having his breakfast as he rushed along the road to work. But we soon discovered this wasn't an unusual sight in this city where life seemed to be lived at running speed.

The other surprising thing was the way nobody seemed to go to bed. I was asked to do some radio phone-ins, one for a couple called Peggy and Eddie Fitzgerald who had had their own show for forty-one years, and another for Dick Sommers. The shows didn't start until John and I would normally have been in bed, and in the early hours of the morning when we were ready to leave, our eyelids heavy as lead, listeners were still phoning in and the presenters were still as chirpy and alert as if it were the middle of the afternoon.

I'd gone to New York mainly to do some television shows and some live appearances at a theatre in Greenwich Village. The first television show was a programme called *AM America* and I was to be given fifteen minutes with the presenter to explain what I did. I thought this a bit strange as I'm used to working with an audience, but I soon realized they probably didn't know what to expect from me. Apparently psychics in New York are usually more interested in foretelling the future than in contacting people who've passed over. There are some extraordinary variations on the fortune-telling theme (apparently you can even have your dog's paw read!), but confronted with a psychic who had no intention of looking into the future – well they didn't know what to make of me.

I was taken on to a cosy set which was decorated to look like someone's living-room. Comfortable armchairs were arranged round a fireplace complete with brass fender, shovels and pokers. I sat down and the interviewer came over and sat opposite me. She was a very attractive, dark haired girl in smart, expensive clothes. She introduced herself as Janet.

'Well, Doris,' she said, 'I know you don't tell fortunes but can you tell me anything about myself?'

Her voice was pleasant but I could tell she was sceptical and my mouth went dry. It's always more difficult to work when people are sending out waves of doubt but the cameras were rolling and they expected me to come up with something. Heart thudding, I tuned in. Instantly all background noise faded away, my field of vision narrowed until I was only aware of Janet and I heard an elderly woman say, 'My name's Mary. I had a cerebral haemorrhage, you know.'

Janet was watching me calmly, a polite smile on her face. I took a deep breath. 'Well, there's an elderly lady here called Mary,' I said, 'and she says she passed on with a cerebral haemorrhage. Have you any idea who she is?'

The effect was astonishing. The colour drained from Janet's face, the smile disappeared and she turned round accusingly to the television crew. 'I just don't believe this,' she said.

Oh God, I thought, I must be way off beam, it's obviously not going to work. I was just beginning to panic when I realized that Janet was still addressing the crew. 'Has anybody been talking to her about me?' she demanded.

I nearly fell off my chair. 'They couldn't have done, Janet,' I interrupted. 'I was taken to make-up the minute

I arrived and then brought straight here. I haven't spoken to any of them.'

The producer agreed that this was correct.

'So you do know Mary?' I ventured cautiously.

Janet nodded. 'Yes,' she said reluctantly. 'She's my grandmother.'

I breathed a sigh of relief. It was going to be all right. The old lady passed on the names of people in Janet's family and then I felt her lean forward and touch the girl's gold wedding ring. 'This is a new one, you know,' she explained. 'She's taken another wedding ring off.'

'That's right,' said Janet. 'I was divorced and I married again.'

The show went on, more and more details were accepted by an increasingly bemused Janet until right at the end I said, 'Mary wants to tell you she's got David with her,' and the girl's eyes filled with tears.

'That's impossible,' she whispered. 'Nobody knows about David. Only my mother and myself.'

'And your grandmother, love,' I said gently. 'David's your son, isn't he?'

'Yes,' she said, and threw her arms around me and gave me a big hug.

Fortunes or no fortunes they were obviously satisfied with my work after that, because the following Friday I was invited back again and this time I was allowed to talk to the studio audience. I wasn't so nervous this time as it was my second appearance but to my horror, when I tuned in, all I could hear was a flood of Italian. It was a woman's voice and very emotional but I couldn't understand a word of it.

When I work with a group of people I see a small light hovering near the person the message is intended for and on this occasion a bright light was dancing crazily over the head of a young girl at the back.

'I want to talk to you, dear,' I said to her, 'but at the moment I can't understand it. I'll have to get it translated.'

I don't know how it happened, but even as I spoke English words started coming into my head over the top of the unintelligible Italian and I knew someone was translating for this excited latin lady.

The light darted round and round the girl as the woman told me her name and then added in a trembling voice, 'She's my bambina, my bambina.' I repeated this aloud, glad to be able to make a start, but instead of answering, the girl burst into tears.

All around me I could sense a buzz of concern. The producer and presenter were alarmed. It must have looked to them as if they'd made a big mistake. They'd trusted me with a studio audience and in less than a minute I'd upset them.

'It's all right,' I reassured them. 'Do you want me to stop, love?' The girl shook her head. I wasn't at all surprised. People often cry at first due to the overwhelming release from emotional tension, but they usually want to hear more.

The Italian lady was still chattering eagerly to me. She gave the name and occupation of the girl's husband who was sitting beside her. Then she mentioned two other people and said to her daughter, 'I'm very grateful to them for caring for you, but remember, I'll always be your mother.'

At this the girl stood up, dabbing her eyes with a handkerchief and explained that her mother was Italian but she remembered nothing about her. She'd been brought up by her adopted parents, whose names her mother had given.

The long lost mother would happily have talked all night but I could hear a babble of other voices clamoring in the background and finally she was nudged to one side.

Immediately, the light bobbed away to the front of the audience and hovered over a group of four or five people sitting together.

'That's Mabel,' said a voice close to me.

'Is one of you Mabel?' I asked. A grey blonde woman with a sun-tanned face looked up in surprise. 'Yes. I am,' she said. And suddenly there was the strong, sweet scent of orange blossom and I was looking at a mass of swaying orange trees.

I couldn't understand this at all. Was she getting married perhaps, but even that explanation seemed obscure. I stared at the picture in my mind, struggling to interpret the hidden meaning. It was no use. All I got was orange trees. I gave up. 'Well,' I said at last. 'I don't know if this will mean anything to you. I can't work it out but all I can see are dozens of orange trees.'

The woman laughed in delight. 'It's all right, Doris. I live in Florida and you've just given a perfect description of my garden. It's filled with orange trees!'

Between appearances on *AM America* I was doing live shows at the Players Theater, Greenwich Village. I'd been worried about going to New York because people had warned me that they're tough cookies over there. 'You'll have trouble getting through to them.' But in fact they were lovely – really warm and friendly. I arrived at the theatre on the first night, to come face to face with two huge photographs of myself at the front and my name in lights over the door: *An evening with Doris Stokes.*

John and I couldn't help standing there admiring it and then John took a picture with his instamatic. It might not be Broadway, but my name up in lights was an occasion to be remembered!

I was pleased to see large numbers of young people every evening who listened attentively to what I had to say and asked intelligent questions. One night a young man stood up and said, 'I've just got engaged, Doris.'

'Congratulations!' I said warmly.

'Well, the thing is,' the young man went on, his face turning pink, 'we love each other very much but supposing anything happened to my wife or me and the other one remarried. What happens on the other side?'

This is a difficult point because it seems to vary from couple to couple.

'It's quite complicated, I'm afraid,' I said slowly. 'It seems to be that if you marry again and love the other person just as much as your first partner, but in a different way, then you might all be together on the other side. But if you're not lucky in love the next time and the affinity isn't there, on the other side you will go to the person you have affinity with.'

At this a tall, blonde woman stood up. 'Well how do I go on Doris? I've been married five times!' Everyone fell about laughing, but I could see that she was serious.

'Which one do you love most?' I asked. 'I think it's your third husband.'

'Why yes, it is!' she said in amazement.

'Well that's the one you'll go to. That's the one who'll be waiting.'

These sessions used to last for ages and the audience took such interest in the proceedings that they didn't want to leave. When the show finished they used to rush to the stage and the stage door; they gathered in the dressing room and wouldn't go. The manager got quite cross about it. One night he said to me: 'Doris, would you please go home and then I can close the theatre and we can *all* go home!'

Towards the end of the week, however, he'd changed his mind. He was so pleased to have his theatre full every night instead of only at weekends that he asked me to stay on another week. Unfortunately I had to refuse. I had long-standing engagements in Britain and I had to leave.

It was while we were in New York that I became involved in one of the most disturbing cases of my career. Quite out of the blue we got a telephone call from a Detective Sergeant Bob Harris from the 49th precinct, who wanted to know if I would see someone at the police station. He didn't say what it was about, only that he'd come and pick us up.

He arrived at the hotel on Saturday morning, a big, black policeman with a warm smile and an understanding manner.

'I'm afraid you might be shocked, Doris,' he said helping me on with my coat. 'We're going to the Bronx and although it's still New York it's a different landscape entirely from Manhattan.'

'Oh, I'm fairly unshockable by now,' I said confidently – after all, I'd seen the bag people and the drunks on the pavement; I was getting used to the harsh contrast of rich and poor side by side. Yet as the car bounced towards the Bronx, I began to feel depressed. The potholes that seemed to scar the roads all over the city were getting worse and I clung to John as we lurched along. The towering glass sky-scrapers of Manhattan gave way to crumbling grey blocks and grubby shops with gaudy hand painted signs over the doors. Rusting cars tore through the streets, radios blaring. Litter overflowed the gutters spilling onto the pavements. No street corner or doorway seemed complete without its group of shabby young men chatting aimlessly. We didn't see a single white face and despite the frosty blue sky and diamond bright sun I felt as if I was on alien territory.

The police station seemed positively welcoming in comparison. At least it was familiar. It was just like walking into one of those television detective films. Dark shirted policemen with guns on their hips strode purposefully around, frayed lino covered the floor, coffee rings circled the desks and the walls were papered with yellowing 'Wanted' posters.

Those posters became unnerving after a while. We stood there in the centre of them, waiting for Bob Harris to show us which office we were to use, and dozens of cold staring eyes seemed to follow us accusingly every time we moved. I turned with relief to one of the few notices that didn't bear a photograph and saw that it advertised a raffle. I brightened considerably. Now raffles I understood. I could relate to a raffle.

'Look, John!' I said. 'Just like at home.' I leaned forward to read the rest of the details and then recoiled in surprise. It was to raise money for bullet-proof vests for the policemen.

'Isn't that dreadful?' I couldn't help saying. 'All the shootings that go on here and the police have to raise their own money for bullet-proof vests!' Then I realized the room had gone quiet and I clapped my hand over my mouth in horror. How tactless of me. What was I thinking of? But the few policemen within earshot just grinned to themselves and went on with their work.

'Right, Doris,' said Bob Harris appearing at my elbow, 'the person you're to work with is in the office. Would you like to come in now?'

'Yes, of course,' I said, glad to get away before I got myself into trouble. 'Where can I leave my coat?' It was quite warm in the station and I'd taken off my coat, a treasured fur given to me by my friends in Australia on my last visit. I was immensely proud of it. It was the first fur coat I'd ever had, but Bob Harris eyed it doubtfully.

'I think we'll take it in with us. I don't know how safe it'll be out here.'

I laughed. 'But this is a police station!' Nevertheless he was quite serious, so in we trooped with Bob Harris carrying my coat over his arm.

A small, dumpy black woman with a red headscarf over her hair was sitting alone in the office. She was chain-smoking and the ashtray on the table in front of her was piled high with dog-ends. I could see by her face that she wasn't at all keen on my visit so I asked Bob to stay and take notes. Perhaps his presence would reassure her.

I explained as I always do that I couldn't guarantee anything but it would help if I heard her voice now and then. She seemed to understand so I tuned in and immediately a woman's voice said, 'I'm Helen and I've got May with me.'

'Do you know these people, love?' I asked the woman.

'That's my grandmother and May's my mother,' she replied reluctantly, but even before these few words died away the air to her right seemed to tremble and thicken and as I watched, a little boy materialized. He was a dear little soul with very short dark curls, melting brown eyes and tiny pink palmed hands. He beamed at me and skipped over to the woman's chair.

'There's a little boy here who belongs to you,' I told her.

'Yes, that's right,' she said. The boy leaned close to her, his head on one side.

'I'm Kevin,' he explained proudly. 'I'm six.'

Even as he spoke a picture flashed into my mind. I could see what looked like a rubbish dump with dozens of old cars, abandoned wheels and bits of engine scattered all over the place.

'He was playing on a dump of some kind,' I remarked to the woman and described what I could see.

'No, that's not a dump,' she said. 'It's a place where people park their cars and do their repair work. Kevin used to spend a lot of time there.'

I glanced back at the child. It seemed unwise to let such a little boy wander off alone to a place like that. I wouldn't have allowed Terry to do it when he was small. Suddenly there was a sharp pain round my neck, something was tightening across my throat and my wrists hurt very badly. I gasped and whirled round to Bob.

'This little boy was strangled with piano wire or something similar,' I spluttered.

'Yes, he was,' said Bob.

'And were his wrists tied with wire too?'

'No,' said Bob, 'they were cut.'

I could hardly look at that poor little child. I felt sick. My head was swimming, my eyes misty and as I hung onto the chair wondering whether I was about to faint, the

17

room swirled away altogether. When the mist cleared I was in the place where his body was found.

I was walking down an alleyway between a dingy derelict house and a great heap of rubbish. Rotting boxes and old tin cans slithered down at the slightest movement, rats scuttled amongst the debris and the slimy path was so narrow I had to walk sideways, my back pressed to the wall.

I inched along, wary of rats and then suddenly I was staggering backwards into empty air. Part of the wall behind me had collapsed and I was drawn silently through the opening into the building. It was pitch black inside and an overpowering stench, like the smell of rotting animal carcasses, enveloped me. My eyes stared blindly into the darkness and horrors crawled across my skin. Something evil lurked just in front of me; I couldn't see it but I could feel its presence in the soupy air. The wire was at my neck again, my wrists were blazing with pain and the smell grew stronger and stronger until I thought I'd suffocate. Choking for breath I groped desperately for the opening in the wall. I made out a slice of light in the blackness and I rushed headlong for it and then I was out, breathing clean air again, my eyes streaming in the brightness. From far away I heard Kevin's voice say, 'There were four of them, you know,' and vaguely I understood that he meant there were four wires attached to the one round his neck. Then there was a jolt and I was back in the office again.

Bob was scribbling furiously in his notebook. Kevin's mother was still smoking silently, her face expressionless but as she lifted the cigarette to her mouth her hand was shaking. I realized I was trembling so much that my knees were knocking together and I had to clamp my lips tightly to stop my teeth from chattering. I took a few deep breaths to get myself under control.

'Is this – too upsetting for you?' I asked the woman when I'd managed to calm myself.

She shook her head. 'No, because I already know these things.'

'You call my mother Dooly,' Kevin interrupted. 'That's her nickname.'

Dooly confirmed that this was true.

Kevin then mentioned his brother Tony, his sister Gloria and the name Peter.

'Who's Peter?' I asked.

Dooly explained that Peter was her boyfriend. Then Kevin drew closer to me as if he had something important to say. 'Will you tell Gloria the baby's with us?' he said.

I repeated this and for the first time Dooly showed some reaction. 'No, no, I don't know anything about any baby,' she said sharply.

'Are you quite sure about the baby, Kevin love?' I asked.

'Yes,' he said positively. 'We're looking after the baby now.'

Dooly pursed her lips and shook her head, but protesting voices were pouring into the room and the loudest of all was Dooly's grandmother, Helen.

'You just tell her we do have the baby with us,' she said angrily. 'The baby came over tragically while Kevin was still missing.'

I tried again but it was no use. Dooly flatly refused to acknowledge a baby of any sort and we were getting nowhere. In fact the atmosphere was getting hostile. The only thing I could do was change the subject.

'Can you tell me about anything else?' I asked Kevin. So he talked for a while about the trip to an amusement arcade promised him by the people who'd lured him away. He also named a person responsible for the murder and Bob confirmed later that this person was at the top of their list of suspects but the police hadn't yet collected enough evidence to charge them. Kevin went on to talk about his teacher at school who had been very kind to him and then he said, 'I'm almost seven now. I was just six when it happened and the baby was six months old.'

I didn't dare mention the baby again but fortunately Kevin went straight on. 'Mummy never gave me any flowers at my funeral, you know,' he added.

I glanced at Dooly. 'He says you didn't give him flowers at the funeral.'

She shrugged. 'No, well I couldn't afford it, could I?'

I couldn't imagine such poverty. I'd been hard up in my time but never in such desperate straits that I couldn't have got together a few flowers for my son's funeral. On the other hand, look at the bag ladies. I couldn't imagine being in their situation either but they existed all right. Quickly I pulled my purse out of my handbag. All I had was a ten dollar bill. I wasn't much good with American money but I felt sure she could get some nice flowers with that. I pressed it into her hand. 'Look Dooly, take this, buy yourself some flowers and put them by the side of your little boy's photo. He'll like that.'

'I haven't got a photograph,' she said. 'The police have them all.'

I turned to Bob. 'Surely she can have one photograph, Bob. You're not working on them all, are you?'

'Of course you can, Dooly,' said Bob. 'I'll go and get one.'

While he was gone Helen came back, still protesting that Dooly knew the baby. She was absolutely determined to get through. It seemed very important to her.

'Look love, you don't have to say anything to me or to Sergeant Harris if you don't want to,' I told her, 'but they are quite certain you know this baby. At least admit it to yourself.'

Dooly stubbed her cigarette violently in the ashtray. 'I don't know what you're talking about.'

'But they are convinced,' I pointed out. 'Sometimes things get a bit confused and I might mishear something or make a mistake but in this case it's quite definite. The message is for you and the baby is connected with you somewhere.'

At that moment Bob Harris came back with the photograph and he caught the end of the conversation. He watched Dooly shake her head in denial once more and he let out a long sigh.

'Are you going to tell Doris or shall I?' he asked wearily. Dooly stared sullenly at the floor.

'All right then, I will. Doris, you're right, there is a baby. Before Kevin's body was found, his sister Gloria drowned her baby, six months old, in a pail of water.'

I struggled to keep the horrified expression off my face and Dooly fiddled with the corner of her headscarf. 'Oh well, yes,' she muttered.

There was an awkward silence. 'Well I think that's just about all you can do, Doris,' said Bob. 'You've been very helpful and there's no way you could have known all the details you've given us, but there was one more thing I was hoping for. One small detail that would clinch it beyond all doubt.'

'Well, I'll try,' I said. 'Perhaps it's something they don't want to talk about.'

I tuned in again and caught Helen's voice as she was fading away. 'What is it, Helen?' I asked silently. 'Can you help?'

And back came one whispered word that made me go icy all over. 'Oh no, I can't say that,' I muttered half to myself.

'Say what, Doris?' asked Bob. 'What is it?'

I hesitated. 'Well, I'm sure the grandmother said witchcraft.'

Bob nodded. 'That's what I was waiting for. It was.'

He led us out of the office but I was so dazed I could hardly take it in. Witchcraft! I couldn't believe it. In this day and age?

In the outer office Bob paused to pick up a sheaf of photographs. 'You were absolutely right, Doris. Kevin was missing for some time and his body was eventually found by an old tramp in a derelict building, exactly as you

21

described. This'll explain why you smelled dead animals.'
He handed me a photograph.

My heart seemed to stop as I realized what I was looking
at and I gasped in horror. As long as I live I will never
forget that terrible picture. It showed Kevin as they'd
found him. The poor little mite was hanging suspended
from four wires, his curly head slumped forward on his
chest, his little arms hanging limp at his sides and on the
ground beneath his tiny drooping feet, a circle of mutilated
animal carcasses . . .

I dropped the picture and I must have gone white,
because Bob quickly guided me to a chair and handed me
a cup of coffee.

'It's all right, Doris,' he said. 'We'll go in a minute.'

We gave Dooly a lift home on our way back to the hotel
but I don't think I said a word. That terrible picture kept
springing into my mind. When I looked out of the window
all I could see was Kevin. Eventually we dropped Dooly
outside her house and the car headed back towards
Manhattan.

'You know after Gloria drowned her baby I went round
to see her,' said Bob. 'I went into her room and although
she had a good bed in the corner she'd dragged the
mattress off it and was sleeping on the floor. I said,
"Gloria, what have you got the mattress on the floor for
when you've got a lovely bed there?" and she said, "I want
to be close to the demons. I want the baby and I to be
possessed." She's in a mental home now.'

'But Kevin . . . It was witchcraft – but why?'

Bob shrugged. 'We don't know, but I'll tell you a funny
thing. Those people have a belief that if an elderly person
in the community is ill or has some infirmity, the soul of a
child who is sacrificed will go into the old person and the
infirmity will disappear.'

'Oh what nonsense,' I protested.

'Yes, of course,' said Bob, 'but I know the family quite
well. Before this happened Dooly was crippled with

arthritis, she could hardly walk. You've seen her today, walking perfectly normally. Don't ask me why.'

By the time we reached our hotel I was feeling limp and exhausted. It had been a long day. The horrifying case hung over me like a dark shadow and I felt grubby from the contact with it. I ran myself a deep, hot bath and lay back under the water soaking the nastiness away.

'Aaahhh that's better . . .' I sighed as my muscles relaxed. But then gradually I realized it wasn't better at all. In my mind I could hear rats skittering through rubbish and if I closed my eyes I could see that photograph of Kevin as clearly as if it was printed on the back of my eyelids. In fact now I came to think of it I was feeling distinctly unwell. I thought I might faint and so quickly got out of the bath. I picked up a towel, pulled it round my neck and almost screamed with pain.

'John!' I cried, gently probing the searing flesh. 'I think I've been bitten. Would you come and have a look?' It felt swollen and sore. Whatever could have done it?

'Honestly, love . . . bitten by what?' said John strolling into the bathroom. Indulgently he lifted my hair to look at the place I indicated, and then he froze. 'My god . . .' I heard him whisper. For there across the back of my neck was a thin red line, a quarter of an inch deep, sore and angry just as if a wire had been put round it and tightened . . .

CHAPTER 2

There was no doubt about it, I was feeling sorry for myself. I hadn't long come back from America, there was Christmas to look forward to and the prospect of moving into a new flat. Nothing grand of course. It was identical to our old flat in the disabled ex-servicemen's block and only a few doors further along the same corridor but it was being modernized and by the new year it would have a bathroom – a luxury I'd almost forgotten. Then in the spring my first book, *Voices in My Ear*, was being published.

Yes, the future was looking marvellous, but instead of feeling happy, I was depressed. Soon after returning home I'd developed a severe pain in my right side. At first I dismissed it as some kind of bug and I was careful to eat plain food and drink plenty of water. The diet didn't help. Instead the pain increased. John, who is a healer, gave me spirit healing every night, which eased the pain considerably but I was still conscious of a grumbling ache every time I moved and a stiff, dragging feeling when I walked.

One afternoon I limped awkwardly back from the kitchen where I'd been making a pot of tea and as I lowered myself gingerly into the armchair a voice said sternly: 'You must go to the doctor, you know.'

I looked round, but of course there was no-one there. Terry was at work and John was out shopping. 'Go to the doctor,' said the voice again, so loudly that I couldn't pretend I hadn't heard. It was a clear warning from the spirit world and deep in my heart I knew that it shouldn't have been necessary. Commonsense should have made me seek the doctor's advice without prompting as soon as I'd realized that in this case John's healing was only going to dull the pain, not cure the problem. I had to admit that I was being silly because I was afraid. I'd had cancer twice before and now any persistent pain that refused to respond to home remedies filled me with dread.

That's the trouble with cancer, even when you're cured. You can't understand what triggered it off in the first place so you can't help wondering whether the same force might be silently at work again. Not that I'm afraid of death, I know there's nothing to fear and as far as I'm concerned they can throw my body into the dustbin like a pile of old clothes because that's all it is. It's just the manner of going that worries me, and as I sat there staring blindly into the fire, the pain sharpening in my side, I couldn't help remembering that my poor father had passed in agony with cancer of the bowel.

Of course I succeeded in making myself thoroughly miserable with lurid pictures of me gone and John and Terry wandering around the dusty flat in creased shirts with only beans on toast for supper, when the shrill ringing of the telephone brought me back to reality.

Begrudgingly I dragged myself to my feet and stumbled out into the hallway, banging my toe on a chair leg as it had grown dark while I brooded and I hadn't switched on the light.

'Hello!' I said into the receiver not as charmingly as I might.

'Hello. Is that Mrs Doris Stokes?' asked a chirpy, bright voice.

'Yes,' I said in resigned mood.

'Mrs Stokes, this is the United States Embassy.'

I blinked stupidly at the receiver. 'The what?'

'The US Embassy. We've been asked to trace you by General Omar Bradley. He is a five star General and one of the heroes of the second World War.'

The throbbing in my side and toes ceased miraculously and I was quite speechless.

'The General and his wife are coming to London to attend the unveiling of a plaque at St Paul's,' the voice which I now recognized as American continued, 'and they would very much like you and your husband to take tea with them at Claridges.'

'I'd love to,' I gasped. 'But why me?'

'Apparently they saw you on a television show,' said the voice. 'The David Suskind Show. They were very impressed and wanted to meet you.'

'Oh . . .'

'They'll be so glad you can come. We'll send you the details by post.'

John walked in as I was putting the phone down.

'Hallo love. Why aren't you resting?'

'I was,' I said impatiently, 'but the American Embassy phoned.' I saw his eyebrows go up. 'They want us to go to tea with General Omar Bradley and his wife.' I could see that he wasn't taking this in properly. He opened his mouth to speak. 'Go and sit down,' I told him. 'I'll put the kettle on and tell you all about it.'

I was amazed at such a response from the David Suskind Show. It was recorded during my visit to New York and I hadn't been at all pleased with my work that day. I didn't feel I'd done a good job.

David had asked me to do a telephone sitting for him before deciding whether to have me as a guest on his show and I assumed he approved of my work because the invitation went ahead. But just before the show started he put his head round my dressing room door. 'I don't want you to be too good,' he said, 'or we shall be accused of collusion.' He was gone before I had a chance to ask him what he meant.

What a funny thing to say, I thought, as I finished combing my hair. Most television people wanted me to be as good as possible, in fact they were usually nervous in case I was a flop and spoiled the programme. I was still puzzling over it when I went onto the set, and a few minutes work left me utterly bewildered.

David gave me a terrible time. As I worked he stood in the audience with a microphone and he kept coming back to the platform, putting his foot on the bottom step and saying, 'Well, how did you do that, Doris? What's the secret?' and questioning almost every message I gave, implying that it was some sort of trick.

I ploughed on but it became increasingly difficult. At one point David was standing next to a young man in the audience and the light hovered between them. The voice was a bit blurred but I could just make it out. The trouble was I couldn't be sure for which of them the message was intended.

'I can hear the name Davis. I think it's Joyce Davis. Do you know anyone of that name?' I asked.

'I know a Joyce Davis,' said the young man guardedly. What they didn't admit was that she was David's wife and she was in the audience, so I was trying to give the wrong message to the wrong person, and of course it didn't fit. So it went on – the waves of hostility from David combining with waves of panic from me, until the voices were obscured in a fog of doubt, and I thought, oh dear, I'll have to pack up, this isn't working at all.

I was just wondering how I could walk off the stage without looking too rude, when a young woman suddenly stood up, took the microphone and said, 'David, why don't you sit down and shut up? You haven't done your homework. You don't know what it's all about. We've come here to listen to Doris. Why don't you let her get on?' And to my horror the rest of the audience joined in shouting, 'Yes, shut up. We want to hear Doris.'

I stood there petrified. The show had come to a standstill and it was my fault. I'd been told that David was a big cult figure in America and I felt sure he wouldn't stand for this sort of treatment. I looked across at him expecting to find him angry, but, suave as ever, no emotion showed. He put his hands over his ears, pretending to be deafened and as the din quietened he said, 'All right, all right, I'll sit down and shut up.'

There was a commercial break just then and the

producer came hurrying over. Oh well, I've done it now, I thought expecting the worst but, to my surprise, he asked if I would do the next hour of the show, if David agreed not to interfere. What could I say? I agreed but I was in such a nervous state my concentration had gone. I did the best I could but I was disappointed. I knew I could have done a lot better under different circumstances and I felt the audience hadn't got as much from me as they deserved. Yet strangely enough I received a lot of letters as a result of the appearance and the Bradleys enjoyed it enough to seek me out.

The prospect of tea at Claridges cheered me enough to go to the doctor but, as I'd feared, I was referred to a cancer specialist. He examined me and I could tell he wasn't happy. 'I think we ought to have an X-ray,' he said. 'I'll make an appointment for you at the hospital and you'll have to collect a bottle of laxative the day before.'

This sounded pretty depressing to me and it got more depressing when I received the appointment. I was to present myself at the hospital at 2 pm on Friday and I was to take the laxative at 2 pm the Thursday before – which happened to be just two hours before our tea at Claridges.

'John, I can't possibly!' I cried when I received the letter. 'Can you imagine what would happen?' But cancer or no cancer, I didn't want to put off our visit. If I was seriously ill I might as well enjoy myself while I could. I rang the hospital and explained my predicament to the sister. 'I'd very much like to go to this tea,' I said. 'Would it be all right if I took the laxative at 6.00?'

'Oh yes,' she replied, 'we make provision for people who work during the day but you'll probably be up late at night.'

'I'll put up with that,' I said thankfully and that's the way it was left.

The days passed, the tea drew nearer and then the Embassy rang again with another tempting invitation. After tea, the General and his wife would like us to join them in the Royal Box to see *Evita*, the famous musical. Could we go?

In anguish I phoned the sister again. 'Oh dear,' she said when I explained, 'I can understand your not wanting to miss out on this. The only thing I can suggest is that you come out of the theatre in the intermission and take the medicine then. But you must go straight home and you'll be up all night.'

'That's all right, sister,' I said rashly.

I had no idea what I was letting myself in for, but it was worth it. I had my hair done and put on a smart day dress, John wore his best suit and we took a taxi to Claridges. John and I had imagined the tea would involve just us, the General and his wife, but to our surprise we were shown into a large drawing-room full of people.

Our feet sank into drifts of deep pile carpet and we stood there a little awkwardly, awed by the elegant furnishings. Instantly an elderly man in a wheelchair excused himself from the group of people he was talking to and expertly manoeuvred himself over to us.

'Good afternoon. I'm General Bradley. Very pleased to meet you.'

We shook hands. He was a fine old gentleman with silvery white hair, a little frail now perhaps, but his eyes were bright and shrewd and his manner alert. Somewhat at a loss for words, I remarked that there seemed to be a lot of military people present.

'Oh yes,' agreed the General. 'They're travelling with me. We've taken over the whole floor of the hotel.'

Just then his wife Kitty came over. She was breathtakingly slender and as elegant as the room.

'Oh there you are, Doris!' she cried. 'I'm so glad you could come. Come and meet some of the others.'

She introduced me to Sir Winston Churchill's grandson, and to Eleanor Hibbert, otherwise known as Victoria Holt, one of my favourite novelists. Apparently Kitty had been particularly keen for Eleanor to come because one night, back home in America, Kitty had been reading one of Eleanor's books, and had become so engrossed in it that she had stayed up to finish it. Hours later the General was taken seriously ill and had Kitty not been awake to attend to him he might have died.

'So you see, if it hadn't been for Eleanor's book I might have lost him,' said Kitty.

We settled down to talk about books while John, who was a paratrooper at Arnhem, had the time of his life reminiscing about the war with the military people. Tea was passed round and though I was only allowed plain bread and butter because of my X-ray the next day, I thoroughly enjoyed myself.

After tea the crowd dispersed, the General was taken away for a rest before the theatre and Kitty asked me if I felt well enough to do a sitting for her. The ache was nagging away in my side as it had been for weeks now, but as long as I sat still and didn't rush about it was bearable.

'I'll gladly try, Kitty,' I said, 'but I can't guarantee good results even when I'm in the best of health.'

'That's all right, I quite understand,' Kitty assured me.

She took me up to her private suite, and Eleanor, who had shown great interest in my work over tea, came along as well to see what would happen.

I think they were quite relieved when I explained I didn't need dimmed lights or candles or any spooky stuff of that sort. 'Just relax,' I told them. 'That's all I'd like you to do.' We sank back in the luxury armchairs, and the silence in the warm room made my eyelids grow heavy. I shook my head impatiently – this was no time to feel sleepy – and then a sweet woman's voice with a soft American accent murmured somewhere near me, 'I'm the General's wife.'

Startled, I stared at Kitty. She was Mrs Bradley and she was still quite definitely on the earth plane.

'The General's wife, dear? Are you sure?' I asked silently.

The woman laughed. 'His first wife, Mary.'

I hadn't realized the General had been married before but Kitty confirmed it. 'Well, Mary says she wants to thank you for all the happiness you've given him. The last thing she wanted was for him to be lonely and miserable and it makes her very happy to see what you're doing for him.'

I think Kitty was a little surprised though pleased with this message, but in fact it wasn't unusual. Where there has been real love between a couple, the one who passes first is usually only too thankful to see her partner happy again with someone new. Remarriage doesn't detract from the original love at all and on the other side that love continues, but free of sexual jealousy.

The sitting progressed. The General's brother came back, followed by some of Kitty's relatives. Then a different voice interrupted loudly with the name, 'Wisconsin.'

I knew this was a place in America. 'I'm getting the name Wisconsin,' I explained. 'Do you know anyone there, Kitty, or do you have any ties with the town?'

She wrinkled her forehead, trying to recall any connection. 'No,' she said at last, 'I don't know that place at all.'

But the voice was most insistent, repeating the name Wisconsin and adding that a baby would soon be born there.

Kitty shook her head. 'No, I'm sorry, that means nothing to me.'

I shrugged. 'Oh well, never mind, we must have a crossed wire somewhere. She doesn't know you,' I added to the voice. 'Can you give me any more . . .'

There was a slight cough behind me and we turned, startled to see that the special sergeant who had been on guard duty outside the open door had come in.

Noiselessly he crossed the thick carpet and bent to whisper something to Kitty. She listened with a puzzled expression on her face at first, but as he finished she burst into peals of laughter. 'No!' she cried merrily.

31

'Oh yes, ma'am,' said the sergeant smiling broadly and went back to his post.

'Well, Doris, I can hardly believe this,' said Kitty when he'd gone, 'but Specialist Rogers just told me that he's from Wisconsin and his wife's expecting a baby next month! We must be giving our sergeants too much time off!'

After the sitting Kitty and Eleanor went to change for the theatre and I was rather embarrassed when they came back in evening dress, because of course I was still in my ordinary day clothes, but they didn't seem to worry. We made our way down to the foyer where the General's aides were organizing transport to the theatre. John and I were to travel with Lieutenant Colonel Little, we were told, and we went outside on to the hotel steps to wait for him. There was quite a party assembling and a line of sleek black cars glided towards us.

'Look at that, John!' I cried. 'We're going in a caval-cade.'

The first car, a long, low affair that shone like glass with a flag fluttering on its bonnet, stopped beside the Bradleys and while they were being helped inside, another Colonel came over and touched my arm.

'Mrs Stokes ma'am. The General and Mrs Bradley would be very honoured if you would ride with them in the Embassy car.'

I gazed longingly at the beautiful car. 'Oh John, would you mind very much if I did?'

' 'Course not, you go. I'll be all right with Lieutenant Colonel Little.'

So I slipped in beside Kitty and almost disappeared up to my neck in pale upholstery. The car whispered away from the hotel and the evening took on a glamorous, dream-like quality. London, during the day when you're pushing through unfriendly crowds and dicing with death from taxis at every corner is one thing, but on a cold night, from the depths of a luxury car, when all the lights are glittering in the darkness and the buildings look warm and inviting, it's quite another. What with the flag billowing proudly on the bonnet and the people staring in the windows at us, I felt like royalty.

The feeling was reinforced when we reached the theatre and were dropped at a side door to find the entire cast lined up to meet us. Dazed, I shook each outstretched hand and then followed Kitty along the carpeted corridors to the Royal Box. It was like a small room with a balcony at the front and chairs arranged in rows. We were so close to the stage I almost felt I was taking part in the show. The only thing that struck me was the draught. After about twenty minutes the cold air was swirling round my feet and I began to feel quite chilly. I thought of the Queen in those flimsy dresses she often wears to the theatre and my admiration for her increased. She must be frozen at times but she never turns a hair.

During the interval we were led to a softly lit retiring room.

'I wonder if the Queen uses this room?' I asked, looking round at the dressing table where drinks were set out and the plush chairs grouped round a low table decorated with flowers.

'Oh yes, when she comes to this theatre,' I was told.

Drinks were passed round and John meaningfully showed me his watch.

'Do you really have to go, Doris?' asked Kitty as John went off to find my coat.

'Yes, I'm afraid I must,' I said reluctantly. 'I'd love to see the second half but I've probably stayed out too late already.'

I felt like Cinderella leaving the ball as I tore myself away, and the glamour of the evening disappeared as if it had never been. Within half an hour John and I were climbing the concrete steps to our flat. Matey the ginger cat was running to meet us, complaining loudly that he was hungry, and indoors the bottle of bitter medicine awaited me.

The sister had been right. It did keep me up all night and I arrived at the hospital next day feeling a wreck. Mind you, that was nothing to the way I left, after an enema and a highly unpleasant X-ray. But I was very fortunate. When the results came through the specialist was surprised to find no growth. I didn't have cancer after all. I was delighted and tremendously relieved of course, but still worried. The pain continued to burn in my side. There had to be something wrong.

Eventually a gynaecologist diagnosed that I needed a hysterectomy as soon as possible. The trouble was I would have to wait at least six months to have the operation performed on the National Health and in the meantime I could hardly walk. If I was prepared to be a private patient the whole thing could be over in a couple of weeks. John and I exchanged glances and I groaned inwardly. We'd saved some money to buy furniture when we moved into our new flat, but now . . .

'Well, it's more important for you to be healthy than to look at a bit of carpet,' John pointed out and of course he was right.

I don't remember much about my stay in hospital. I know it was run by nuns who were very kind to me, but one strange thing happened that stands out in my memory.

After the operation I struggled to open my eyes. My head felt stuffed with feathers and my throat was dry as sand.

'Don't worry, dear,' said a voice from somewhere above me as cool hands fluttered near my face, 'we're putting a mask on to give you some oxygen to help you breathe.'

It was water I wanted not oxygen, I tried to tell them, but then I drifted away again and the next time I opened my eyes I felt more comfortable but couldn't remember where I was. To one side I could see a pair of unfamiliar

34

french windows and to the other . . . my eyes widened in surprise, a handsome young man in naval uniform.

He stood there beside my bed, so smart with his dark hair and close fitting blue jacket with its gold buttons and braid round the sleeves, and as he smiled at me I recognized him: it was my war time friend Walter Pryce Jones!

But what am I doing in Wales? I thought weakly as I struggled to smile back; I was far too tired to speak. Then I remembered. I wasn't in Wales, I was in hospital in London and Walter had passed over years ago.

Even as the thought slipped through my mind, Walter walked to the foot of the bed, smiled encouragingly at me once more and disappeared . . .

CHAPTER 3

I first met Walter Pryce Jones when I was in the WRAFs stationed in Port Talbot in Wales. I'd just come off duty one afternoon and I was waiting for a bus to take me into town when a little Welsh lady at the bus-stop started talking to me. She had dark wavy hair and kind eyes.

'How d'you like Port Talbot?' she asked.

'Very much,' I said. 'I've never been to Wales before.'

'And how d'you get on up at the school? Are you comfortable there?'

Our HQ was in the vicarage and the WRAFs were billeted in the school. 'Oh yes, we're very comfortable,' I said. 'They look after us very well. The only thing I ever miss is a bath. They've only got showers at the school which are all right, but there are times, when you've been on duty all night and half the day, when the one thing you long for is a nice hot bath.'

'Then you must come and have a bath at my house,' said the lady immediately.

I felt my face burn red. 'Oh, no – I mean – I wasn't asking . . .' I was dreadfully embarrassed. I'd been chattering thoughtlessly again and put my foot in it. 'I couldn't possibly . . .'

'Of course you could,' said my new friend firmly. 'I'd like you to. It'd be nice to have some company. My son's in the navy so I don't see much of him these days.'

And that's how I met the Pryce Jones family. Walter, Mr and Mrs Pryce Jones' only child, became a great friend. There was nothing romantic about it, he was going out with one of the other WRAFs, but he had a marvellous sense of humour and he could always bring me down to earth with his common sense when I was in a tizzy about

36

some scrape I'd got myself into. Like the time I was in trouble for disobeying a superior officer . . .

I was working as a WRAF driver and one evening when I was on night duty I was asked to pick up one of our officers from the General Hospital and take him to the military hospital. It seemed straightforward enough but when the man came out I noticed he only had slippers on his feet, although it was his arm that had been injured.

'Where are his shoes?' I asked the sister who helped him into the back of the car.

'Oh, they must be at the police station,' she said. 'I think they were round his neck when he hit the tree.'

This seemed rather strange to me, but the man obviously needed shoes, I could see that, so I stopped at the police station to fetch them for him.

When I came out again, the shoes under my arm, I was a little disturbed to see that the officer had moved into the front of the car. Oh well, perhaps he wants a chat, I thought nervously, and got in beside him without comment.

It was 3 am by now and very dark indeed, particularly as the headlamps were taped to allow only half an inch of beam, but I knew the road well and soon we were spinning down the black country lanes. We were making good time, when suddenly I heard the leather passenger seat creak, and an instant later the man lunged at me. He only had one good arm but he could manage well enough with that and he was very strong. He pulled me towards him and as I tried to beat him off with one hand and steer with the other, the car was swerving all over the road.

I can only assume he'd been drinking. 'Oh – look – be careful, sir, we'll crash!' I cried in alarm, but he only laughed and tried to drag me out of my seat. The wheel spun through my fingers, I could see a tree looming out of the blackness in front of us and I was terrified.

Pushing him away with all my strength, I wrenched the wheel round again, my brain racing. The man was clearly

37

enjoying the whole episode. I could feel his breath on my cheek and he closed in again. I'd have to do something, fast. I made an effort to block the fear and anger from my voice.

'We'll have to get to the hospital first, they're expecting you,' I gasped as sweetly as I could manage. 'We can stop on the way back,' and I gave him what I hoped was a playful kittenish push. It worked. The man chuckled and settled back in his seat, but I had to endure his arm round my shoulders for the rest of the journey.

At the hospital I helped him out of the car and then dashed on ahead up the steps. One was supposed to book oneself in and out of the hospital and, much to the amazement of the sergeant on duty, I booked myself in and then straight out again.

'Hey, just a minute,' he cried, as the officer came up behind me, 'you might have to take him back again.'

'Not me, sergeant,' I said backing down the steps, 'I've had enough.'

At that moment the officer realized that he'd been tricked. 'Hey!' he shouted, stepping towards me. I jumped the last three steps with the officer right behind me.

'Come back here, driver! Come back this minute!' he yelled, but I was in the car. The engine fired, I did a racing U-turn and as I accelerated away the last furious words, 'I haven't dismissed you yet . . .' came floating through the window.

'You'll be lucky, mate,' I said under my breath and for some reason I was overcome with the wittiness of this retort and giggled all the way home.

The next day of course I was in a terrible state. I realized I'd done a very silly thing but though I went over and over the events in my mind I couldn't think of any other course of action I could have taken. I was too young to know how to handle the situation. In terror, I went to see Walter, who happened to be home, to ask his advice.

'Don't worry, Doris,' he said when he'd heard my story,

'it's serious on the face of it but I should think that officer would be far too embarrassed to complain about you and even if he did, you need only tell the truth and he'll be in trouble, not you.' Then he burst out laughing at the thought of me wrestling with the wheel and a burly officer at the same time. 'I must say though,' he spluttered, 'you mustn't make a habit of it, but good for you, Doris. I bet you taught him a thing or two!'

I couldn't help laughing myself. Walter was like the brother I never had. He made me feel much better.

Two days after that I was arrested for disobeying an order from a superior officer, but Walter was right. After I explained in great detail what had happened to several officers in ascending rank, the matter was dropped and I heard no more about it.

Several months later I popped in to see Mrs Pryce Jones as I often did on my way back to the billet. Over a big pot of tea she liked to tell me all the gossip of Port Talbot and then she loved to hear my stories of life at the school with the WRAFs. On this particular day as I walked into the hall, the sitting room door was open and I saw Walter in his uniform cross towards the fireplace.

'Oh, I didn't know Walter was home on leave,' I said as I unbuttoned my coat.

'Walter?' said Mrs Pryce Jones in surprise. 'Walter isn't home, dear. Whatever made you think that?'

And I looked again and saw that the living room was quite empty. A terrible pang shot through me. I knew nothing about spiritualism or mediums in those days, but several strange things like this had happened to me, usually with tragic results. Oh God, no, not Walter, I thought in despair and Mrs Pryce Jones must have caught my stricken expression.

'Why, what's wrong dear,' she asked, her mother's face suddenly white with fear. 'What made you think of Walter?'

I forced myself to smile. 'Oh nothing,' I said lightly,

taking off my coat. 'Maybe I've got a crush on him and I see him wherever I go.'

A few weeks later I had to go home to Grantham because my mother was ill but I'd only been back a fortnight when I received a desperate letter from Mrs Pryce Jones. Walter had gone. The day I'd seen him in the living room, his ship had been torpedoed and Walter was lost at sea. Mr Pryce Jones had had a stroke only a week before the official letter came through and she didn't know how to break the news to him. Could I come down at once?

I could only get a forty-eight hour pass and the old steam trains were a lot slower than our modern expresses today. Forty-eight hours barely gave me time to get from Grantham to Port Talbot, stay the night and go back again, but of course I went. I was very apprehensive about my task. I sympathized with Mrs Pryce Jones, but if she didn't know how to tell her husband, how could I? And yet in the end, from somewhere, the words came. I remember kneeling by Mr Pryce Jones' chair, holding his hand as the tears trickled down his poor old cheeks, telling him over and over, 'Walter hasn't gone, Mr Pryce Jones. Not really. You will see him again. I know you will. Don't ask me how I know, I just know you will.'

That was the strange thing, even in the days before I was a medium, people used to seek me out in their grief, as if they knew instinctively that I had the means to comfort them. The same thing happened a few years later when my friend Edie was going through a difficult time.

By then I was married, I understood more about spiritualism and I was no stranger to grief. I'd lost my own darling baby, John Michael, at 5 months 2 weeks while my husband John was a prisoner of war.

In those long black days following John Michael's death, I was convinced the sun would never shine again, not for me. But of course it did. John came home, we adopted little Terry and we settled down in Grantham among my old friends.

Edie Clark was one of the best. Small, dark and vivacious, she'd been my friend since we were children together in the same street, and we've remained friends ever since.

In those days there was a marvellous community spirit in Grantham. Everyone helped each other. When Edie, her husband Jack and their three little girls, Joan, Susan and Beryl went on holiday, Edie would get them ready and do the packing on Friday night so that on Saturday morning, all she had to do was give me their door key. I used to look after their dog, collect up the dirty washing, wash it, iron it and put it away. Then I'd go in every day to check that everything was all right and the day before they came home I'd clean the house and get food in for them. It was second nature because that's the way we lived then and of course Edie did exactly the same for me.

Christmas Day was a particularly exciting time. Edie would start first because with three ecstatic little ones waking each other up and bursting to know what Father Christmas had brought them, I expect she was up at the crack of dawn. I'd hear them early on Christmas morning laughing and giggling as they skipped down the street with Edie and Jack strolling behind. Then there would come a thunderous knocking on the door and in seconds our living room was submerged in wrapping paper and happy people as the children exchanged presents from the tree and Jack, Edie, John and I had a glass of sherry.

That was only the beginning. After a while we'd move on to wish a merry Christmas to another friend, where the procedure was repeated, then she would join us and we'd all go on our merry way to the next house and so it went on until by lunch-time we were a very jolly band wandering home to serve the Christmas dinner and if there were a few extra people at the table, what did it matter – it was Christmas after all.

Like me, Edie had known tragedy. Her only son, Tony, had died in hospital during an operation to remove his

41

tonsils. Something went wrong, they said. So when her youngest daughter, Susan, had to have the same operation Edie was understandably frantic. I sat with her during the long hours while we waited for the operation to be performed but the staff at the hospital were very good. Knowing the family history, they telephoned Edie as soon as the operation was over to let her know that it had been a success and that Susan was quite safe.

Sure enough, within a couple of weeks Susan was back home again as fit as ever and making her sisters jealous with exaggerated tales of the mountains of jelly and ice cream she'd eaten in hospital. She was a slim, pale child of 7 with soft, curly, fair hair. She was much quieter than the other two. When they called for Terry, Susan was always the one who hung back shyly and it was Susan who lost her tongue when strangers were near. She loved to listen to stories and she was never happier than when she was drawing. While her sisters were playing boisterously on the floor, Susan would sit for hours at the table working away with coloured pencils, her fair hair flopping across her face, the tip of her pink tongue showing between her teeth.

One beautiful summer day, a month or two after Susan came out of hospital, we decided to take the children for a picnic at nearby Denton reservoir. It was a spur of the moment idea. Edie and I cut a stack of sandwiches and filled the flasks with tea for the picnic basket while the men gathered towels and swimming things.

We had a marvellous afternoon. We didn't need money to enjoy ourselves in those days. The children ran races on the grass and darted in and out of the water. Then John and Jack chased in after them and there was a tremendous splashing match, children against Dads, resulting in squeals of delight and showers of water.

Edie and I sat on the bank, dangling our legs in the water and watching them happily. The sun was warm on my face and as I looked up at the cloudless blue sky and then round at the other families scattered across the grass playing ball or running with dogs I couldn't help thinking that this was perfection. The war was over at last and this was what life was all about: children and parents playing together on a summer's day.

The sun was bright, we were all happy and no-one sensed, not even me with my clairvoyant powers, the shadow that lay across the afternoon.

At tea-time Edie and I towelled the children dry and changed the girls back into their cotton dresses and Terry into his shorts. Then we opened the picnic basket, and every sandwich was devoured hungrily. Afterwards there was an unruly ball game, while Susan collected daisies to make a chain.

'What d'you think, Auntie Doris?' asked a small voice as I was stuffing Terry's damp swimming trunks into a bag ready to go home. 'Do I look nice?' and I turned to see Susan standing there, one creamy daisy chain round her neck, another in her hair.

'Like a princess, love!' I told her. 'Go and show your dad.' A flush of pleasure pinkened her cheeks and she danced away to find Jack.

The following Saturday Edie went shopping in town, leaving the girls with her mother who still lived in Turner Crescent – my old street when I was a child. By the time she returned, Susan was complaining that her legs hurt and she couldn't walk. Edie had to piggy-back her home.

Jack called to see me shortly afterwards. 'Could you come and see what you think, Doris? I expect she's only tired but you know how Edie worries.'

When I got there Susan was in bed. She didn't look too bad but her forehead was hot to the touch.

'I think you'd better get the doctor, Edie,' I advised. 'She's running a temperature.'

'That's what I thought,' said Edie anxiously.

I waited while the doctor came and gave Susan some medicine, then I went home to cook John and Terry's tea.

43

At eight o'clock that night Terry was in bed, the dishes were cleared away and John and I were just settling down to listen to the wireless when there was an urgent knocking on the door.

'Whoever can that be?' I muttered as I got up, but even before I reached the door I knew it was Jack. His hair was dishevelled, his tie had slipped sideways and he looked frightened.

'Would you mind coming again, Doris?' he asked. 'There's something wrong, I'm certain of it.'

An unpleasant thought was trying to gather at the back of my mind but I pushed it away fearfully and hurried out after Jack. Edie met us on the doorstep. She was biting her lip nervously.

'She seems worse now, Doris, but the doctor was only here a couple of hours ago. I don't know whether to bother him again or not.'

I ran up the stairs into Susan's room. The little girl was tossing and turning in the bed, her hair damp on the pillow, her face flushed, her breathing noisy. Automatically I put my hand on her forehead, though it was quite obvious she had a high temperature. As my fingers brushed her skin, a jolt went through me like an electric shock! Susan was going to die. I knew it as certainly as if it had already happened. Horror and pity struggled inside me as I stared down at that thin little figure under the bedclothes. Edie was hovering at my shoulder, wringing her hands in distress.

'What – what d'you think, Doris?'

I couldn't look her in the face. 'You must get the doctor at once, Edie,' I said quietly without taking my eyes off Susan. 'She's very poorly indeed.'

The doctor returned, took one look at the way Susan had deteriorated and had her rushed to hospital.

When I got home that night John was waiting up for me. 'It's bad, is it?' he asked, seeing my miserable face. I flung myself into a chair, suddenly feeling tired and old and hopeless.

'It's dreadful,' I said. 'I don't think Susan's going to make it.'

'Oh don't say that, love.'

'It's not an opinion, John. I knew almost as soon as I looked at her,' I said wearily.

John and I were both becoming involved in spiritualism by then and my powers as a medium were just coming to light. John knew enough about it to take my premonitions seriously.

'Well let's hope you're wrong,' he said.

'Of course I hope I'm wrong,' I snapped, tired and depressed. But I knew I was right.

The next day I hurried to the Clarks and I was surprised to see a knot of neighbours hovering outside the gate, their faces gloomy yet inquisitive.

'You're not going in there!' someone cried as I approached the door.

I turned. 'Of course I am. Why shouldn't I?'

'They've got polio in there!' said someone else.

'Polio!'

Shocked, my hand went rigid on the knocker. So that was it, polio. Poor Susan. I turned back to the neighbours. 'And what difference does that make?' I snapped angrily and I rapped defiantly on the door.

There was nothing I could do of course. I just wanted Edie and Jack to know I was there sharing the burden with them as much as possible. Joan and Beryl had been sent to their grandmother and Susan was undergoing an emergency trachiotomy to help her breathe. But it was no use. Within 24 hours she was dead.

Poor Susie, poor Edie, poor Jack.

I thought they'd never get over it. For a while Edie blamed herself. If only she hadn't let Susan go in the water that day, if only she'd kept her at home, if only . . . It's a heart-rending and useless way to think of course, and we pointed out to her time and time again that the others had gone swimming that day with no ill effects. No one could possibly be blamed for what happened to Susan. Yet I understood how Edie felt. I'd been exactly the same after my little John Michael's death.

John Michael died after an emergency operation to remove a blockage of the bowel but the official cause of death was pneumonia. For months afterwards the cruel thought nagged me that the baby in the next cot also had pneumonia, and he survived. That baby was the youngest of nine and compared to John Michael, had been carelessly reared.

If I hadn't been so particular with John Michael, I tortured myself endlessly, he might have had more resistance to germs. But no, my baby had to be spotless. I suppose with John away, a prisoner of war, I had nothing else to do but tend my baby obsessively. Also, my first job after leaving school had been in a hospital where they impressed on me very young the need for high standards of cleanliness and hygiene. It never occurred to me that the standards needed in a hospital where patients were recovering from operations and where infections could be fatal, were not necessarily required in an ordinary home of healthy people. So I washed and bathed my baby continually and nagged my mother. 'Put on a clean apron before you pick the baby up,' I'd insist and though she'd grumble, 'A little bit of dust won't hurt him,' she'd do as I asked.

We lived near a railway station and after he was washed and dressed I used to put John Michael outside in his pram if the weather was fine. But if he got one speck of black on him from the steam engines, in he would have to come and off would come his things and I'd wash him again. 'Honestly!' said Mother, watching me disapprovingly, but she didn't interfere.

After he passed, the matron in the hospital came to see me and thinking to comfort me, I suppose, remarked, 'We've never had a baby in such perfect condition. There was not a mark on him, not a speck of nappy rash or anything.' But I only sobbed more violently. What was the use of a perfect corpse?

By the time Edie and Jack were suffering their terrible tragedy, John Michael's death had driven me to find out more about spiritualism and recognize my own powers at last. I was taking my first faltering steps as a medium, but I never did do a sitting for the Clarks. Jack wasn't keen on that sort of thing and I was wary of pushing my beliefs onto anyone else. I would have loved to share my peace of mind with them but I had to respect their distaste for the subject. Instead I gave them what comfort I could.

Edie would come and cry in my kitchen and I'd make her tea, put my arms round her and promise her over and over again, 'The sun will shine again, Edie. I know it will.' And, of course, eventually it did. Joan and Beryl grew up into fine, strong young women and presented their parents with healthy grandchildren. Jack and Edie think the world of them, but as Edie said to me recently, 'You never forget do you, Doris?'

And I had to agree, no you don't ever forget . . .

CHAPTER 4

I went back to Grantham a few months ago, shortly after the local paper had printed a story about me, and as I was walking down the street an elderly man stopped me.

'It's Doris, isn't it?' he said. 'I don't suppose you remember me, do you?' And though his pleasant open face looked vaguely familiar I had to confess that I didn't. 'I used to be the landlord of the Spreadeagle. Your mum used to help us wash the glasses,' he reminded me. 'Oh, but Doris – that bit in the paper – wouldn't Jenny have been proud of you if only she'd lived to see it? She'd have been so proud about all this.'

I didn't have the heart to tell him that Mum did know all about it because she still keeps an eye on me. It was very nice of him to bother to mention it – but would Mum really have been proud of me if she was still here on earth? Somehow I doubt it because she always seemed quite incapable of understanding what I did. Whether it was genuine incomprehension or whether she simply closed her mind to it, I don't know, but her complete bafflement was brought home to me, once and for all, the time I took her to a spiritualist meeting.

After meetings in our local hall, the group I was involved with used to sell tea and biscuits for a few coppers to raise money for a visit to another group some distance away. A coach was hired, tea was provided for us by the host group and the occasion was quite a festive afternoon out.

On this particular occasion I had been invited to speak at a meeting quite a long way off. A coach was hired and as it was a pretty journey and I knew Mum loved coach trips I asked if she'd like to come. She wouldn't bother with the spiritualist bit, I realized that, but she'd be given a nice tea afterwards and taken home again, and all in all I thought it would be an enjoyable outing for her.

Mum agreed. 'Oh, yes Dol, I'd love to go,' she said eagerly and immediately started pondering which hat to wear.

Everything went smoothly. The weather was fine. We picked Mum up from her home in Fletcher Street and got her a window seat on the coach. She was thrilled with the route through rolling countryside and once at the hall, she sat most politely through the proceedings. True there was a highly puzzled expression on her face, I could see that even from the platform, and she kept turning round as if trying to see who I was speaking to, but at least she didn't scoff or express loud disapproval as I'd feared she might.

Afterwards she was taken off for tea and by the time I found her again she'd made a couple of friends. She was sitting between two middle-aged ladies, cheerfully sipping her tea.

'All right, Mum?' I asked joining them.

'Oh!' gasped one of the women, staring at me as if I'd just materialized out of thin air, and then turning to the other two as if I wasn't there, she said, 'Isn't she marvellous? I think she's marvellous.'

'Who?' asked Mum.

'The medium, of course,' said the woman in hushed tones.

'Medium?' said Mum. 'What's a medium?'

The woman looked at her in disbelief. 'The medium's the one who's been talking on the platform all afternoon,' she said a little uncertainly as if fearing it might be a joke.

'Well I didn't see any medium,' said Mum firmly, going back to her tea. 'There was only one person up there and that was our Doris.'

I couldn't help laughing. Dear Mum. If she lived to be a hundred I'd never make her understand.

When I was a child, of course, she was quite well aware of my strange 'unnatural' streak and did her best to stamp it out with dire warnings that I'd end up in a mental home one day. But as I grew older and became independent she chose to forget about it and once she made up her mind about something, nothing would shake her. The subject was closed.

She lived next door to a Pentecostal church and she used to make tea for the pastor. He knew I was a spiritualist and we often had friendly but heated discussions about the rights and wrongs of it. This used to distress Mum. She'd follow the conversation backwards and forwards for a bit, a bewildered expression on her face and then she'd say, 'Now pastorman's a good man, our Doris. You shouldn't talk to the pastor like that.'

'It's all right Jenny,' the pastor would reassure her, 'we're not falling out.'

But Mum was quite determined. 'He's a good man, the pastor,' she'd tell me sternly, 'and he's a *pastor*!' and that would be the end of that discussion.

Mum was a living contradiction. Black haired and small – she only came up to my shoulder – she could be timid as a mouse or embarrassingly forthright. When I was in the WRAFs, if I dared linger on the way home for a kiss and a cuddle with a boyfriend and it was after eleven at night, Mum would come to find me, and I was twenty-four at the time. Round the corner she'd appear like a bad dream, her stockings rolled down round her ankles, a broom in her hand.

'You can pack that up, our Doris!' she'd shout. 'It's time you were home.' And she'd stand there, broom at the ready, while the embrace dissolved, quite prepared to beat the unfortunate boyfriend about the head should he refuse to put me down.

She could be very stubborn and she was a push-over for status and labels. Just as she didn't think I should argue with the pastor, because he was a *pastor*, she never really got over my rejecting an officer to marry a sergeant. So incensed was she about my marriage to John, that she refused to come to the wedding and she was cool towards him for many years afterwards. When we adopted Terry, she was totally against it, and declared that she wouldn't allow him under her roof because he wasn't our natural born son. Then a few months later, with one of her famous about turns, she accepted him so wholeheartedly that if John or I so much as slapped him for being naughty, she'd go berserk.

'I'll fetch the police to you,' she'd shout. 'I will, I'll get the police. Leave him alone, you're not to slap him!' Of course it didn't take Terry long to learn where to go for sympathy and sweeties.

She was alone for a long time was Mum, because my father passed when she was only in her late forties, but she kept herself busy and everyone liked her. After the initial shock of father's death, several people tried to persuade her to marry again. It would have been a good idea, I suppose, because Mum was hopeless with the business side of life. Anything to do with money had her wringing her hands in despair, yet give her someone to clean and polish for and she was in her element. But she just wasn't interested in other men.

The only time I can recall her giving in to persuasion was when her friend Flora Hudson talked her into having a perm and going out for the evening. I must have been fifteen or sixteen at the time and I remember being absolutely astounded at the sight of Mum coming downstairs in her best dress with her hair a halo of crisp curls and wearing lipstick for the first time in her life.

'And what d'you think you're staring at, our Doris?' she asked sharply as she came into the kitchen, but the self conscious patting of her hair gave her away. 'Well, what d'you think?' she relented, peering doubtfully at her rigid hair-do in a tiny handbag mirror. 'Does it suit me or was I a fool to listen to that Flo?'

'It's very nice, Mum,' I said kindly. 'I was a bit surprised, that's all.'

And off she went for her evening out, tugging at her dress and chewing uneasily on the unfamiliar lipstick.

It didn't last of course. Try as Flora might, Mum just wasn't the type and soon the perm grew out, the lipstick gathered dust in the drawer and Mum spent her evenings at home with the wireless.

She might be a bit touchy with us at times but Mum was really a softie with a heart as big as a bucket. She could never say no to anyone and consequently she had several little jobs that she did regularly as clockwork because she hated to let anybody down. For a few shillings a week she helped out at the Spreadeagle pub, scraping and cleaning the vegetables and washing the glasses. She took great pride in every task, no matter how small and her vegetables were always spotless, not a mark on them and she polished the glasses until they sparkled like cut crystal. 'I've never had a washer-upper like your mum,' the landlady used to tell me with admiration.

They were pleased with her at the fish shop too. They'd give her her supper and in return she washed their tea towels and carried the takings to the bank. She became a familiar sight trotting through Grantham with the leather bag of money on her way to the bank but no one ever bothered her. It never crossed our minds to think it could be a dangerous journey. It wasn't like that in those days. Mum would never get rich on her little jobs, but then that didn't worry her. As long as she wasn't in debt she was happy and the little she had she was just as likely to give away.

I remember getting cross with her about it one afternoon. I'd popped round to see her and finding her out, I went round the back to wait. There in the yard, I came face to face with a middle-aged woman filling a bucket with coal from Mum's coal bunker.

'What d'you think you're doing?' I demanded angrily.

'Oh, your mother lends me a bucket of coal, you know,' said the woman continuing to heap her bucket.

52

'Well you just put it back and wait till Mum's here,' I said furiously. John didn't earn much because his war injuries prevented him from holding down a decent job, so I had to go out to work to help support the family and half the time I also paid for Mum's coal because she was always broke.

Reluctantly the woman emptied her bucket and we stood there glaring at each other in silence, until Mum finally returned. I wasn't too surprised to learn that the woman had been telling the truth. Mum did allow her to help herself to coal whenever she needed it. So I had to stand by while she smugly refilled her bucket and carried it triumphantly away.

'Well, you see her husband's not very good to her,' said Mum as the gate clicked shut.

'And what's wrong with her going out and scrubbing floors or something like I have to?' I retorted, but it was no use. You couldn't change Mum and deep down I wouldn't have had her any other way. It did mean that I was frequently called upon to come to her rescue, however, and in those days I'm afraid I was less patient than I am now.

On another occasion I dropped in to see her unexpectedly and found her sobbing at the table.

'Whatever's the matter, Mum?' I cried, rushing to her side. 'What's happened?'

'Oh, nothing, nothing,' she snuffled, wiping her eyes on her apron. 'I just feel so poorly this afternoon, I don't know how I'm going to get through this washing and I've got to finish it today.'

I looked down and for the first time noticed the most enormous bundle of dirty sheets and clothes heaped on the floor.

'Mum, that lot can't possibly be yours,' I said in surprise and then bit by bit the story came out. The woman up the road took in lodgers and for a couple of shillings and a bar of soap, she'd persuaded Mum to do all the washing and ironing for her.

'Why on earth didn't you say no?' I asked in exasperation.

Mum picked helplessly at the hem of her apron. 'I didn't like to. She's got so much to do with the cooking and the house and everything.'

I sighed. It was pointless even asking. 'All right, Mum, leave it to me,' I said wearily and picking up the huge bundle I staggered out into the street. Fortunately the address mum had given me wasn't far away and I knocked boldly on the door.

There was a pause, then a solidly built woman in an apron appeared.

'Are you Mrs So-and-So?' I asked.

'Yes,' she said.

'And you take in lodgers?'

'Yes, that's right,' she said, obviously thinking she had another customer.

'Then do your own dirty washing,' I cried angrily, 'and don't go giving it to my mother to do!' and I'm sorry to say I thrust the bundle at her so hard, I nearly knocked her over.

Before he died, even though I was only thirteen, my father had asked me to take care of Mum and over the years I did my best. I tried to sort out her problems, I visited her regularly, made sure she had enough money and coal and every morning, when I was preparing lunch for John and Terry before I left for work, I made up an extra meal for Mum, put it in a covered basin and took it with me. She used to meet the bus and I would hand over that day's lunch and she would return the previous day's basin. That way I knew she had at least one balanced meal a day.

But looking back over the years, I know I did fail Dad at one point and to this day I feel guilty about it. It was in the months following John Michael's death and I'm sorry to say that I was so wrapped up in my own grief I never spared a thought for Mum and what she must have been feeling. During the five months of my baby's life, we lived with Mum and she loved John Michael like her own son. She was so proud of him, she loved to show him off to the neighbours and looking back I realize she must have felt as lost as I did. At the time the thought never crossed my mind. Selfishly I decided I couldn't stay in the house that held so many painful memories so I moved in with my friends, the Webbs, leaving Mum all alone in her grief.

Afterwards I discovered that she and her neighbour, Mrs Scothen, used to sit together and cry in the evenings, while I went out with my girlfriends to drown my sorrows.

I was only once knocked out of my selfishness. Early one evening I was getting ready to go out. I was standing at the mirror in the Webbs' kitchen making up my face when the air raid sirens started to wail. I dabbed defiantly at my nose with the powder puff. Well, I wasn't going to the shelter now. Let those Germans do their worst. What did I care if I lived or died anyway? I was still carelessly applying powder when planes whined overhead, and I heard the whistle of falling bombs and then there was the most appalling crash. My whole body jarred, the floor rocked under my feet, the mirror swung on the wall and from somewhere I could hear the sound of shattering glass. Outside guns were chattering at the sky, the planes droned on and the crashes continued like receding thunder.

'God,' I said to my startled reflection, 'that was close!' And as I stared in fascination at the strangely white face and eyes grown huge and dark, I realized that I didn't want to die after all.

I was still standing there muttering stupidly to myself when Stan Webb, who was a special constable, rushed in.

'Doris!' he shouted as he tore up the hall: 'They've fallen on Fletcher Street!'

My heart plummeted. 'Oh my God! Mum!' I cried. The powder compact dropped from my hand and pushing past Stan I raced outside and tore up the road. It was pitch dark because everyone observed the blackout, not a street lamp or lighted window shone and once or twice before my eyes became accustomed to the dark I stumbled and twisted my ankle. I turned painfully into Commercial Road and a haze of dust and smoke seemed to hang in the air. There was a peculiar scorched, burning smell and as I glanced to my left my feet slowed down as if they were moving through toffee. The familiar serrated skyline of rooftops and chimney pots had gone. A row of three storey houses had been razed to the ground. One of them had been the home of an old school chum of mine whose mother was a friend of Mum's. I found out afterwards that the little boy had gone up the passage to look at the searchlights and they never did find anything of him at all.

The full horror of that gaping hole in the night took a few seconds to sink in and then I remembered. 'Mum!' I cried aloud and I took off again faster than before.

Fletcher Street didn't look as bad as Commercial Road. Torchlights were bobbing in the darkness and dazed people were emerging. Mum's house was still standing but the roof had caved in. Shaking with fear I pushed open the door and ran down the dark passage. There were voices. I could definitely hear voices, I realized, and I burst into the kitchen in delight. An amazing scene greeted me. The place was full of people, candles flickered everywhere revealing fallen plaster and cracks in the ceiling and in the midst of it all, hair and eyebrows white with dust, was Mum – making tea. She glanced up from the kettle and saw me standing in the doorway.

'What have you come for? You don't want to be in this lot.'

'Are you all right, Mum?' I asked breathlessly.

'Of course I'm all right,' she said peevishly, shovelling great scoops of tea into the pot. 'You can see I'm all right.'

Rather taken aback I stood there helplessly looking round at the smoking candles and the tightly packed neighbours. I realize now that Mum must have been suffering from shock and she was doing the only thing she could – making tea. Anyone who diverted her from this compulsive task was a nuisance.

'Well, I just came to see if you were all right,' I repeated.

'Never mind me,' she said, 'what about the Burgess family in Commercial Road?'

'I know, I've seen it,' I said miserably.

'Well, you go home, our Doris. You don't want to be in this lot. There's nothing you can do.'

She was right. I hovered a little longer, getting in the way and then I wandered back to the Webbs. On the way I couldn't help reflecting that I'd neglected Mum lately. I'd been so wrapped up in myself I'd hardly thought of her. Supposing her house had suffered a direct hit like the Burgesses'? I'd never have had a chance to make amends. Well, I'd been given a second chance and I decided to make good use of it.

I didn't always remember my good resolution, I have to admit. There were many black days when depression closed in like black fog and I was incapable of doing anything for anyone; but as the months passed I returned gradually to normal, and on balance, I think I kept my promise to Father.

She kept well, did Mum. She lived to 73 and over the years she suffered little illness. The end was sudden and unexpected.

One morning about eight o'clock the doorbell rang and I found a little boy on the step. He was Mrs Scothen's nephew and he'd ridden round on his bike with a note for me. 'Could you come down right away? Your mum's very poorly,' Scottie had written. A knot of apprehension twisted inside. Mum wasn't getting any younger. What on earth could be wrong?

'All right, love, thanks very much,' I told the boy as brightly as I could. 'Tell your Auntie I'll be down as soon as I've got Terry off to school.'

I hurried back indoors and bustled John and Terry through their breakfast. 'I don't know what's wrong, John,'

I told him as I collected up the porridge plates, 'but if I'm going to be out for some time I'll send you a message.'

I buttoned Terry into his school mac to save time, though he was quite capable of doing it himself and protested furiously. Then I dragged him to the bus stop, saw him safely on the bus and hurried round to Fletcher Street.

I found Mum in the kitchen, doubled up with pain, her face shiny with cold sweat. Scottie was there beside her trying to persuade her to drink a cup of tea.

'You'll feel a lot better for a hot drink, love,' she insisted. 'Now come on, just try a little.'

Mum was shaking her head fiercely and declaring she felt sick. No matter what the weather, Mum was in the habit of going out early every morning to fetch Mr Scothen's paper for him so that he could read it with his breakfast. When she hadn't appeared Mrs Scothen had called to see if anything was wrong.

'She's been up all night with pain,' Scottie told me anxiously. Mum didn't seem to hear. 'I'm sorry I haven't been to get Mr Scothen's paper,' she was muttering over and over again. 'I did mean to get it.' She seemed really worried about it.

'Blow Mr Scothen's paper,' I said. 'Let's see what's the matter with you.' But I knew she was really ill, so I got her into bed, tucked her up with a hot water bottle and went out to phone the doctor.

Some time later after a long examination, the doctor came out of the bedroom with a prescription. 'It may only be a severe tummy bug,' she told me, 'and in that case this medicine will help, but if she doesn't show any improvement, or if she gets any worse, telephone me immediately.'

I fetched Mum's medicine from the chemist, cleaned the house and refilled her hot water bottle. She seemed easier by then and was falling into a doze so I went home to prepare Terry and John's lunch.

When I returned in the afternoon I was shocked at the

change in her. Her face was grey, she was soaked in sweat and she was vomiting badly. I could see she was desperately ill.

'Now don't worry, Mum,' I told her as calmly as I could, 'but I think I'll go and phone the doctor again. She said she'd like another look at you.'

I moved unhurriedly through the house but once outside I flew down to the telephone box. 'You'll have to come straight away,' I told the doctor when I got through. 'My mother's very ill indeed.'

This time there was only a short examination. 'Oh dear,' said the doctor, 'I'm afraid we'll have to get your mother to hospital.'

Mum, however, had other ideas. She wasn't going to budge, she insisted, until she'd had a strip wash. She wasn't going dirty to hospital and that was it. What sort of person did we take her for? Whatever would the nurses think? Although she didn't have a bathroom it was her custom every morning to put a bowl of hot water on the kitchen table and have a thorough wash and woebetide anyone who called before nine o'clock when she finished.

'Get me some hot water, our Doris,' she said firmly, though she must have been in agony because it turned out that she had a strangulated hernia. So I boiled a kettle and took the steaming bowl into the bedroom.

'I'll do it, Mum,' I said setting down soap, flannel and towel beside the bowl.

'Oh, no you won't. I'm quite capable. I'm not in my dotage yet,' Mum snapped but rather weakly. And she hauled herself painfully to the edge of the bed and meticulously scrubbed every inch of her body, only calling me back to help with her feet because she couldn't bend down to reach them.

We took her to hospital then and they operated on her at eleven-thirty that night. When I phoned they told me she'd come through the operation and was as well as could be expected. I was tremendously relieved. I'd had a nasty feeling this would be Mum's last illness and it wouldn't have been surprising, after all, if at her age she had failed to survive the operation.

When I went to see her she was feeling pretty rotten and her chest was bad but she didn't look too poorly. She was obviously depressed, however.

'Well that's it, our Doris,' she announced as soon as I'd shown her the oranges I'd brought. 'I shall have to come and live with you. I can't live on my own any more.'

And much as I loved my mum, my heart sank. Oh no, I thought, it would be a disaster. She could be so difficult at times; reprimanding John and I over the smallest offence, letting Terry get away with murder, digging in her heels stubbornly over some minor detail and yet being amazingly careless over something important. How could we cope? I forced a bright smile onto my face.

'There's no need to worry about it, Mum,' I said. 'We'll always take care of you.'

And of course we would. My mind ticked over the details. We only had two bedrooms and one living room. Mum could hardly sleep downstairs in that. There was nothing for it but to move Terry's bed into our room and put Mum in his. It wouldn't be comfortable, but we'd manage somehow.

Towards the end of visiting time Mum's eyelids began to droop and I decided to leave her to get some sleep. 'See you tomorrow,' I whispered. 'Have a nice sleep,' and I crept away.

The next morning I was peeling potatoes when there was a knock at the door. Drying my hands on my apron I hurried to open it and came face to face with a uniformed policeman on the step. My heart flipped over and my knees felt watery. It was John Michael all over again. I sagged against the door frame.

'Mrs Stokes?' he asked.

'Yes,' I mumbled, my mouth dry.

'Could you come to the hospital? Your mother's danger-ously ill.'

For a moment I didn't know what to say. My brain was racing in confusion and the years turned backwards. Was it John Michael who was ill or Mum, or maybe both of them?

'Mrs Stokes?' The policeman had stepped forward in concern. 'Are you all right? You did know your mother was in hospital, didn't you?'

'Oh yes, yes,' I said and my mind locked into practical-ities. John! I must get a message to John. 'I wonder if you could do something for me, officer? Could you tell my husband? He's a gardener and he's working on the green in front of the town hall.'

'Certainly, Mrs Stokes,' said the policeman. 'Glad to help.' He trudged away and I tore off my apron, dragged on my coat and raced round to Edie.

'I've left a stew on,' I told her after I'd explained what had happened. 'Could you give Terry his dinner for me?'

'Of course, Doris,' said Edie. 'You get along to the hospital and don't worry about Terry. I'll look after him. I hope your mum improves.'

I smiled gratefully at her and then I rushed off, buttoning my coat as I went. By the time I got to the hospital John was there. He squeezed my hand quietly and we went into the ward together. We found Mum propped up on a pile of pillows to help her breathe, her chest rasping painfully. Her skin was papery yellow but she was conscious.

'Hello, Doris,' she wheezed. Then she noticed John and her voice sharpened. 'What's John doing here? Is there something the matter?'

I didn't know what to say. 'Well, he thought he'd pop in to see you,' I muttered lamely.

Mum wasn't fooled. 'But they've only just had their dinners. What's he doing here at dinner time? He should be at work.' There was silence as John and I both struggled to think of a plausible explanation. Before either of us could reply, Mum added, 'Am I going to die then?'

I hesitated. Faced with a direct question like this what could I do? Should I lie? Was it fair to lie? Didn't she have a right to know the truth? Down the years came my father's voice: 'You must always tell the truth, Dol. You can't go wrong if you tell the truth . . .' It was as clear as if he'd been standing behind me. That's what he wanted me to do.

'Well it's quite possible, you know, Mum,' I said slowly. 'You've got a bad chest and you've just had a big operation.'

If anything, she seemed relieved. She relaxed back onto the pillows and let out a long sigh. 'Oh well, I'll just go to sleep if I die, won't I?'

'Yes, you will,' I said gently. She lay quiet for a moment, then she looked up at John.

'I'm so sorry,' she said softly but quite distinctly and then she closed her eyes and fell asleep.

Those were the last words she ever spoke and I'm so glad they were to John. For so many years he'd felt unaccepted and even disliked by my mother because she considered he'd 'stolen' me from a man of higher rank. Yet it was John who went to her house uncomplainingly to do little odd jobs for her, it was John who first noticed when she needed new, comfortable shoes and it was John who in the later years cut her toenails for her when she could no longer reach them. He had never shown any resentment about it, but I know it meant a lot to him to hear at the end that Mum had forgiven him and that she realized she'd made a mistake.

I sat with Mum for the rest of the day, only leaving her bedside to phone my half sister, Edna, who was living in London, to break the news and tell her to come at once.

The next day I returned to the hospital and the chair by Mum's bed. She never regained consciousness. The long hours dragged by as if time had been suspended. I never took my eyes off that still figure in the bed. At intervals the kind nurses offered me food but I couldn't touch it. My mind was spinning in confusion.

Of course I knew that Mum couldn't live forever but I hadn't expected the end to be so sudden. Only four or five days ago she'd been trotting about doing her odd jobs as healthy and fit as a woman fifteen years younger. That was a blessing really, I supposed, but it made her sudden deterioration all the more shocking. I found myself thinking back to my childhood and the time when my father was alive. Those long evenings when I sat at the table drawing endless pictures entitled 'My Family' with a great tall male figure, a tiny little woman tucked protectively by his side and two little girls close by. Every now and then Mum would glance over my shoulder as she cleared away the supper dishes, but we were very quiet, both listening to father who sat by the fire telling us stories as we worked.

How long ago it all seemed now. Yet this time, sad though I was, I didn't suffer the same shattering grief I'd felt over the loss of my father and John Michael, because by now I was a medium, I understood more of what life was all about and I knew that Mum wasn't really dying. She was going on to be reunited with my father. Poor Mum. She'd been on her own for so long, she'd be so glad to be back with her Sam.

Some time during the evening I glanced at the window and noticed it was dark. Edna must be nearly here, I thought, turning back to Mum, and then I gasped. I could see her spirit body poised face down over her physical body and as I watched, it started to rise. I leapt to my feet, hurried down the ward and found a nurse. 'Could you come quickly,' I asked. 'My mother's near the end.'

Without comment the nurse followed me back through the beds to Mother. 'Oh yes,' she said at once, 'I can see she is. We'll move her into a side ward.'

I hovered anxiously while they bustled about in that subdued way they have in hospitals, keeping one eye on the pale spiritual body that was floating away from Mum. They wheeled the bed out of the ward with me at their heels, into a small single room and as they were making Mum comfortable, I glanced up and through the glass partition, I saw Edna in the corridor.

'Edna!' I cried darting outside. 'Come on, Mum's in here!'

Edna was looking pale and harassed, her pretty blonde hair hastily combed off her face. To my surprise, instead of moving, she hugged her winter coat more tightly round her and hesitated awkwardly. Then I remembered that Edna, like Mum, was squeamish about anything to do with illness or death. Just entering a hospital was very difficult for her.

'You can see Mum from the door,' I said more kindly. 'You don't have to go right in.'

So Edna popped her head round the door and then quickly withdrew.

'You can go and sit in my room if you like,' said the sister who was passing and saw our difficulty. So we trooped up the corridor, settled ourselves in the tiny office and the waiting began.

At one point the sister came back. 'Why don't you go home,' she said. 'There's nothing you can do.'

'Oh, yes. Let's go home,' said Edna half rising from her seat. I shook my head.

'She'll quite possibly go through till tomorrow morning, you know,' the sister added persuasively.

'She won't,' I said firmly. 'I'm staying. You can go if you want, Edna, but I'm staying here.'

Defeated, Edna sank down again. 'Oh well, if that's the way you feel, I'll stay with you.'

The sister went out and the hours dragged by again. The hospital was very quiet. The visitors had long gone, the meals were finished for the day and it seemed as if everyone was asleep. Then suddenly we heard sharp footsteps clacking briskly up the corridor. Tap, tap, tap,

64

tap, tap, they went, coming closer and then they stopped outside our door.

'Oh, my God!' cried Edna fearfully. 'They've come to fetch us!' She jumped up, opened the door – and there was no one there. Puzzled she poked her head out and looked up and down the corridor but it was quite empty.

'I don't understand,' she said coming back. 'I *heard* those footsteps.'

'So did I,' I replied. I was staring at the empty doorway in a fuddled, sleepy way and then with a shock like a dash of cold water my brain cleared. Footsteps . . . someone coming to fetch us – someone who couldn't be seen . . . Mum! I leapt to my feet. 'I must see how Mum is!' I cried to Edna over my shoulder and I raced back up the corridor.

The door to the side ward was propped open and as soon as I walked in I could see I was only just in time. The silver cord, like an umbilical cord which attaches the spirit body to the physical one was stretched to its full extent and my father was there. I couldn't see him but I could feel his presence in the room. He was standing at the foot of the bed and he was talking to Mum. 'It's all right, Jen,' he was saying. 'I'm here. Don't worry. Sam's come to take care of you. You're all right now.'

I saw a nurse passing down the corridor and I dived to the door. 'Nurse. My mother's going!'

'Oh no, Mrs Stokes,' she said coming back. 'The doctor hasn't long been in and he says she'll last the night.'

'I'm sorry, nurse,' I insisted impatiently, 'it's happening now.'

With a resigned sigh she walked in past me and then stopped abruptly. 'Oh, my God. I'll get the doctor!' and she hurried away. But it was too late. Even as her footsteps echoed down the corridor, Mum sat up, gurgled once, the cord parted and she was gone.

Mum would have been very pleased with her funeral. It was a grand affair. Stan Webb, who was an undertaker, arranged for the passing bell to be tolled. Mum would have liked that. Whenever she heard the sombre 'dong, dong, dong' of the passing bell she'd always say, 'Somebody important's passed over then.'

Well it rang loud and clear for her and as the cortège wound up Commercial Road to St John's church, all the curtains were drawn in the street. The church was packed. Even the bank manager and his wife came and quite a few other 'important' people.

It would have made Mum's day to see all those fur coats turned out for her – in fact it probably did!

CHAPTER 5

It was a terrible day. Sleet was falling, the damp, icy cold seemed to seep right into your bones and I was huddled over our gas fire surrounded by boxes.

It must have been about the worst possible day we could have chosen to move flats. I'd only just come out of hospital and I was so weak, exhausted and sore, that the most I could manage was to dust our ornaments, wrap them in paper and pack them away. Fortunately our friends and relatives rallied round to help John and Terry move the furniture down the corridor into our new flat.

Matey crouched miserably in his basket. He didn't like all this bustle and fuss, he wanted to stay where he was. I chatted soothingly to him as I worked.

The emptying flat was beginning to look rather forlorn with light rectangles on the walls where pictures used to hang and gaping spaces where furniture had stood for years. We'd had many happy times in this flat and I was sad in a way to be leaving it. I was particularly sorry to be leaving my rose, but it was impossible to take it with us.

It was very strange that rose. A couple of years before, both John and Terry had forgotten my birthday. Now, my birthday comes very soon after Christmas and I know it's a difficult time so I don't expect presents, but cards mean a lot to me. John and Terry had always been very thoughtful in this respect, but for some reason, this particular January, they both forgot.

It had never happened before. I didn't say anything but I felt unloved and sorry for myself. Every time I looked at the bare mantelpiece a pang went through me and in the end I took myself moodily into the bedroom where I wouldn't have to look at it. It's not fair, I muttered; I work and slave for them, see to their every need. How would they like it if I forgot their birthdays? And so I went on, convincing myself I was thoroughly hard done by. After a while I realized it was getting late and with a martyred sigh I went out to start dinner.

As I moved into the living room something bright caught my eye. I stopped and glanced back. It had been something on the wall, something glinting where nothing had glinted before. And then I saw it. Raised from the plain white wall, like an embossed pattern was a perfect, long-stemmed gold rose. My mouth fell open. I had chosen that colour scheme myself. Just plain, bare walls painted white; clean and simple and easy to wipe, the way I wanted it. Gingerly I put out my finger and touched the rose. It felt just like embossed paper. It was as real and substantial as the rest of the wallpaper.

'John!' I called, my birthday sulks forgotten. 'Come and look at this.'

He wandered in from the kitchen. 'What?' I didn't say anything, just in case the rose was my imagination. I simply pointed at the wall.

'Good God!' said John seeing it at once. 'Where did that come from?'

I shook my head. 'I don't know. I'm sure it wasn't there this morning. I would have noticed it when I was dusting. I just came out of the bedroom and there it was.'

John leaned forward and began inspecting the rose closely. He too put out a timid finger and ran it lightly over the flower's raised surface. Nothing happened.

'D'you think it could be a pattern from the wallpaper underneath coming through?' I asked.

'No. The decorators scraped if all off before they put this lot on,' said John. He stared at the rose in wonder. 'I can't understand it.'

I decided a scientific approach was called for so I fetched a knife from the kitchen and carefully scraped away a piece of paper at the side of the rose. Sure enough, the wall underneath it was clean and bare.

68

There was still one test I wanted to make and a few weeks later I was able to make it. Going shopping one day I came upon our decorators at work on another flat. 'Excuse me,' I called putting my head round the door.

The foreman came over. 'Yes, madam?'

'I know it's a little while ago now,' I said, 'but do you remember decorating Flat 55?'

'Yes, very well,' he said cautiously.

'Well, can you remember if you stripped the walls right down before painting them?'

'Oh yes,' he said. 'We always strip right down to bare plaster before we put anything else up.'

'So there's no old wallpaper left in the lounge?'

'Not a scrap,' he assured me. 'Why, is anything wrong?'

'Oh no, nothing at all,' I said and went on my way leaving a very puzzled foreman behind me.

After that my beautiful gold rose became quite famous. Friends often popped in to ask if they could bring their friends and relatives to see it and at times my living room was like a tiny art gallery. I couldn't give my visitors a proper explanation of my rose, but I like to think it was a birthday present from the spirit world to cheer me up when everyone else had forgotten.

The rose didn't fade. It was still there when we left our flat and I said goodbye to it reluctantly. The chance to move was too good to miss and had cropped up quite unexpectedly.

All the flats in our block were to be converted and modernized with bathrooms installed, but it was a long slow process. First one empty flat was completed, then a family would move in and work would start on their old flat. On completion another family would move into that flat and the process would be repeated. We were right down near the bottom of the list and expected to wait well over a year, but then there was a tragedy.

A few doors along, an old lady lived alone. She was almost blind, poor soul, but she was unfailingly cheerful.

I kept an eye on her when I could. If I didn't see her for a day or two and couldn't get an answer when I knocked on her door I'd alert the nurse. But most of the time the old lady was in good health. In fine weather she'd toddle across the landing to see me as I tended the plants we kept in pots outside our door. She loved a drop of sherry, so I'd go and pour her a glass and she'd sit there happily basking in the sun, sipping her sherry and chatting to me as I weeded.

Then one day when we were abroad, there was a terrible accident. Apparently the old lady got up in the night to put the fire on and caught the hem of her nightie on the bars. The whole garment went up in flames and the poor woman was found burned to death the next day in her smoke-blackened, ash-strewn flat.

We were terribly shocked when we hard the news, but as weeks and then months went by we couldn't help noticing that the flat remained empty. This seemed very strange when there was such a long waiting list for converted homes, but I was amazed to discover that no one wanted that flat. Either they were superstitious about it and felt it was an unlucky place or they were worried it might be haunted. At any rate no one wanted to know, the flat remained empty and we remained near the bottom of the waiting list.

In the end I said to John, 'If nobody else wants it why don't we ask if we can have it? We're not superstitious and I don't mind if the old dear comes back for a visit every now and then.'

John thought this was a good idea. The older we grew the more difficult we found life without a bathroom and the chore of filling the bath in the kitchen was becoming increasingly hard. So I telephoned the secretary of the Foundation and was very pleased to hear that we could have the flat as long as we were prepared to pay for the necessary work and redecoration. In the end it cost us rather more than we'd bargained for, but it was worth it to have a modernized place.

The old lady was quite active in the flat at first. One day I went into the kitchen, partly because I wanted to fetch something but mainly to admire it. I was very proud of my new kitchen with its clean magnolia walls, gleaming white units and smart tiled floor and I stood there beaming round it. Then, suddenly the feel of the room changed and I was conscious that the old lady had come in. There was silence for a few moments and a strong sense of bewilderment, then she said, 'What have you done with my red curtains? They are warm, you know, warm.'

I couldn't think what she meant at first, and then I remembered that before the flat had been decorated I'd found a pair of old red curtains still hanging at the kitchen window obscuring most of the light. I'd taken them down and put up fresh white nets instead.

'Well, dear,' I said as tactfully as I could, 'I like a lot of light and those curtains made the kitchen a bit dark.'

'But red's warm. It's a nice warm colour,' she insisted. Unspoken but strong came the distinct impression that she didn't think too much of my bright, pale decor. Then the feeling faded and I was alone in the kitchen again.

A few days later I came out of the living room and almost bumped into a woman standing in the hall. For a moment I thought John had left the door open and a visitor had walked in without my hearing, but then I saw that it was the old lady. She was wearing the same thick cardigan and tweedy skirt she so often wore as she sipped sherry with me in the sun, and her wispy grey hair framed her face, a little untidily the way it always used to. She seemed to be studying the red carpet and the posters from Australia that I'd pinned to the walls. Then as I watched she wandered towards the bathroom and melted right through the door. I hurried after her but by the time I got there, being forced to go through the door in the conventional manner, she'd vanished. All that was left was an echo of confusion.

I sat on the bath thinking about how it must look to her eyes. I bet she didn't understand it at all. There was the toilet in the same room and same position as before but now instead of blank walls around it there was a shining bath and hand basin. The poor old dear must think she'd come to the wrong flat.

She must have got used to us living there I think because gradually her visits tailed off until the only evidence of her presence was centred around the bedroom, probably because that was the room where her body was found.

One night John went to bed first while I emptied the ashtrays and plumped up the cushions in the living room. It only took a minute or two and when I came back from the bathroom I noticed that the bedroom door was firmly shut, whereas it had been wide open before I'd gone out. Cheeky devil! I thought, he's forgotten me.

'You needn't have closed the bedroom door!' I called to John. 'I'm coming to bed, too, you know, so don't hog all the electric blanket.'

'I didn't close the door,' John mumbled sleepily as I went in. The blankets were up round his ears, he was dozing off and he certainly didn't look as if he'd risen again after going to bed.

'Well, it must have closed itself then,' I said undoing my dressing gown, but as I glanced back at the door I realized this was most unlikely. Designed for disabled people it was wider and heavier than a normal door and when pushed wide open it had a trick of sitting back on its hinges and staying in place so that it wouldn't swing shut on a wheel chair or slow moving invalid. To close it again required a decisive tug and John, in bed, was too far away to administer one.

The mysteriously closed door became a feature of life in our new flat and in the end I came to the conclusion that the old lady, always one to feel the cold, had been in the

72

habit of shutting the bedroom door every night to keep the warmth in. Our apparent carelessness must have worried her and so she closed the door for us when we 'forgot'.

1980, the year we moved into our new flat, was also the year my first book, *Voices in My Ear*, came out and I don't think I've ever been so busy in my life. The book wasn't coming out until May, so I thought I'd have a bit of a rest until then. Which just shows how little I knew about publishing. Apparently monthly, and even some weekly, magazines publish months in advance and in order to write about a book appearing in May, they would have to see me at the beginning of the year.

I'd only just come out of hospital, of course, and was still feeling very sorry for myself but with Ramanov, my guide's help, I was sure I'd get through the interviews. That was something else I had to learn. My interviews nearly always turned into sittings, but I couldn't blame the journalists for asking me to work. It's all very well writing about being able to talk to spirit people, but journalists tend to be curious and rather cynical people and unless I could prove to them that I was telling the truth they weren't likely to believe it.

I did so many interviews/sittings in 1980 I can hardly remember them, but one in particular, probably because it was among the first, stands out in my mind.

The interview with the *Tatler* had been arranged for a date only three or four weeks after I came home from hospital. Brian Inglis, the book reviewer, was coming along with the assistant editor who would have a sitting and there would also be a photographer present to take pictures.

I'd never seen the *Tatler* before so John bought me a copy and as soon as I saw it I don't know whether I was more nervous or excited. It was a glossy high class magazine, more likely to cover stories of aristocratic weddings than of ordinary people like me. I fretted about the state of the flat because I wasn't well enough to look after it myself and I fretted about my appearance which was rather the worse for a major operation. By the fateful morning, however, I'd managed to calm myself and agree that John was right: they'd have to take us as they found us.

The photographer was the first to arrive and when he saw me, his face fell a mile. 'Oh, my God!' he said rather discouragingly I felt, though I could hardly blame him. I was perched up on a rubber ring with my legs outstretched on a pouf.

'Didn't they tell you I'd just come out of hospital?' I asked.

'No, they didn't,' he said looking even less cheerful than before.

'Well, I'm sorry, son,' I said. 'I've done my best.' I was feeling a bit depressed myself by now. I was still so stiff and sore it had taken me two hours to get myself bathed, dressed and put heated rollers in my hair. I'd thought the results were reasonably respectable but obviously I looked worse than I thought.

Anyway John made some coffee, Brian Inglis and the assistant editor arrived and though they looked a bit startled at first sight of the rubber ring they tactfully made no comment and we began the sitting.

I tuned in. Instantly a tiny light swam before me. It was such a faint pin prick that I said to myself, now, am I really seeing a spirit light or is it just a reflection? 'It's a real light, child,' came Ramanov's reassuring voice from a distance. But it's very small, I said silently.

'Yes, he's only just come over,' said Ramanov.

I turned to the assistant editor. 'I've got someone here who's just gone over.'

She shook her head. 'No,' she said.

I stared at the light. 'Yes, it's a man and he's only just passed.'

'No,' she repeated firmly. 'I haven't lost anyone.'

The light still glimmered teasingly before my eyes but I

couldn't hear a thing. Brian Inglis and the assistant editor exchanged glances. They were getting impatient and I was getting cross. I knew the man was there. There was no doubt about it but what was the point of coming to me if he wasn't going to say anything. And what a time to choose! Was it some sort of joke?

'For God's sake, don't mess about,' I told him inwardly. 'This is very important to us all. I've got to prove you're here. Give me some clue.'

'My name – is – Clive,' he said with great effort.

The assistant editor looked blank when I repeated this. 'And he's talking about a girl called Tracey,' I added desperately as Clive blurted out more information, but the woman shook her head again.

This is hopeless, I thought, and then I felt Ramanov direct me to the photographer who was sitting on my left and for the first time I noticed he had tears in his eyes.

'You?' I asked.

His face went white. 'Oh, my God,' he said. 'Clive only died at three o'clock this morning.'

'And who's Tracey?' I asked gently.

'Tracey's my girlfriend.'

I breathed a sigh of relief. Clive was genuinely trying to get through to someone after all. He wasn't being mischievous. The difficulty I had experienced was simply due to the fact that he'd only been over a few hours and obviously found it a struggle to communicate.

'You're doing very well, Clive,' I told him. 'It's marvellous that you can do this so soon.'

He was trying to say another name. 'Su – Su – Suzanne.'

'Who's Suzanne?' I asked.

'Suzanne's the one who rang me at seven this morning to tell me about Clive,' said the photographer.

The light was beginning to fade but I felt that Clive was still trying to tell me something important.

'I want to thank him,' he said faintly, 'thank him for taking the trouble – in his busy life – to drive up to see me.'

75

I repeated this to the photographer. 'Does that make sense to you?'

'Yes, it does,' he said. 'While Clive was ill I used to drive from London to Yorkshire to visit him. I was there last weekend.'

I blinked. The light had gone out. Clive had got his message through and gone. I think the assistant editor found this genuinely interesting but I was suddenly aware that the sitting had been intended for her and she must be disappointed.

I concentrated on her and tuned in. This time there was a response. I got the impression of a man and a sharp pain in my chest.

'There's a man here who passed with a heart attack,' I said.

She nodded at last in recognition. 'My father,' she admitted.

'Tell her I've seen the boy,' he said in a crisp, educated voice. 'She thinks I've never seen him.'

'He says he's seen the boy, love,' I repeated obediently. 'Does that sound right?'

'Oh yes,' she said. 'My son was born after Father's death.'

The man went on to say his name was William but 'Call me Bill, everyone else does. Or you could even call me sir,' he added with a chuckle. I didn't understand this last part, but before I could ask what he meant he took me into a neat, yet lived-in looking sitting room. In my mind I was facing a big window with sun pouring through, then Bill tugged my arm, pulling me to the left so that I could see a photograph on the wall. It showed a squadron leader in full uniform.

'Your father was in the airforce,' I said out loud, 'and there's a picture to the left of the window in his sitting room of a squadron leader. Am I right in thinking that was him in his uniform?'

76

'Yes, that's right, Doris,' said the girl in amazement. 'You're absolutely right.'

'No wonder he's telling me to call him sir, then!' I laughed.

CHAPTER 6

Outside the children's playground Irene MacDonald, mother of the sixteen year old girl murdered by the Yorkshire Ripper, suddenly stopped. She opened her handbag, took out her glasses and bent down to peer at the pavement. She was scrabbling about, examining each paving stone in a preoccupied, distracted way that I didn't understand. I could feel her distress.

'What are you doing, love?' I asked gently, going over and putting my hand on her shoulder.

'I'm just looking to see if the blood's gone,' she said without looking up. 'There was blood all over here, Doris. I just wanted to see that they'd washed it away.'

For a moment I couldn't speak. I just stood there watching that poor tortured woman, busily working over the pavement as if it had been her own kitchen floor, and my heart went out to her. You poor soul, I thought, how this terrible thing has played on your mind.

'Come on, love,' I said helping her up. 'It's all gone now. It's quite clean.'

She came without protest but she still seemed disorientated. 'There was, there were blood stains all over there, Doris,' she kept saying, looking over her shoulder as I led her away. 'You should have seen it. Covered in blood.'

I met Irene quite by chance. In the months before my book was published I found myself caught up in an astonishing blaze of publicity. I'd imagined that all one had to do was write a book, send it off to the publishers and then sit back and wait for it to appear in the shops. Of course it wasn't like that at all.

Tours of Britain, Australia, New Zealand and Tasmania were arranged; there were interviews, television appearances, radio shows; one thing seemed to lead to another.

My feet hardly touched the ground. Of course it was very exciting and in many ways very helpful. Thanks to the publicity, I was able to meet many people, people like the MacDonalds whom I would never otherwise have had the chance to help.

At first I was delighted. Publicity was marvellous, I decided, because it created so many opportunities. It was some time before I realized there was another side to such exposure. Everything has a price, I suppose, and I finally discovered with a shock that the same publicity that made things happen, could also spoil them and leave behind a sour, bitter taste.

The Yorkshire Ripper story is a case in point. Like everyone else, I read about the crimes of the Ripper with horror. As the trail of bloody murders in the North of England grew, I could understand the anger and the fear of the people living in the area and I prayed the madman would be caught. But it didn't occupy too much of my mind. After all, I was very busy with my own life and the murders occurred hundreds of miles away. There didn't seem to be anything I could do to help.

Then one day I was asked to appear on a TV programme in Newcastle on Tyne. I was getting quite used to this kind of thing by now and I had my hair done and packed a smart dress to wear in what was becoming a familiar routine. John and I went to the studios, they got me ready, I was introduced to the presenter and then suddenly, instead of asking me to work with the studio audience as they normally did, they produced a tape recorder. 'I'd like you to listen to this tape and see if you can get anything from it,' said the presenter.

She pushed in the cassette, clicked the switch and the thick Sunderland voice of a man claiming to be the Yorkshire Ripper streamed out. The studio fell silent as the man cruelly taunted George Oldfield, the man in charge of the Ripper hunt, for failing to find him.

'I'm Jack,' he said slowly. 'I see you are still having no

luck catching me. I have the greatest respect for you, George, but Lord, you are no nearer catching me now than four years ago when I started.

'I reckon your boys are letting you down, George. You can't be much good can you?'

I'm Jack, I repeated to myself and I tried to tune into the voice. There was something odd about it. It didn't sound quite right somehow . . .

'The only time they came near catching me was a few months back in Chapeltown when I was disturbed. Even then it was a uniformed copper, not a detective,' the man continued in his slow monotonous drawl. 'I warned you in March that I'd strike again. Sorry it wasn't Bradford. I did promise you that but I couldn't get there.

'I'm not quite sure when I will strike again but it will be definitely sometime this year. Maybe September or October, even sooner if I get the time.

'I'm not sure where. Maybe Manchester. I like it there. There's plenty of *them* knocking about. They never learn, do they, George? I bet you've warned them but they never listen. At the rate I'm going I should be in the Guinness Book of Records. I think it's eleven times up to now, isn't it? Well I'll keep on going for quite a while yet.

'I can't see myself being nicked just yet. Even if you do get near I'll probably top myself first. Well, it's been nice chatting to you, George. Yours the Ripper.'

And at the end of the tape he played a few bars of Thanks For Being a Friend.

I'm Jack, I'm Jack. I repeated the phrase again and again in my mind, turning it round, probing the thing that didn't fit and suddenly it came to me. The man wasn't speaking naturally, it wasn't spontaneous, he was reading a message. His voice was slow and careful at first with all traces of his personality ironed out but towards the end he couldn't suppress little bits of himself creeping in. I got the impression of an intelligent man but very mixed up. I also got the feeling that at one time he could have been a policeman or security man or something similar.

Then over the top of the cassette I heard a woman's voice and she was weeping. She was rather faint because I didn't have a proper link, a sitter to work with, but she said her name was Polly and she'd passed with cancer. I took it that she was probably the man's mother. Anyway, she said the man had been married but was living apart from his wife, his name was Ronnie or Johnnie and the name Berwick featured in his address.

I explained to the presenter and the audience that I had no idea if this information was any use because it is so difficult to get an impression from the voice of someone who's not talking directly to you. Also there was no way of knowing if this man was really the Yorkshire Ripper. Polly had been upset about something but she hadn't said it was murder.

Nevertheless, there were police at the studio who noted it all down and as a result of the broadcast, Irene MacDonald, whose innocent daughter Jayne had been savagely murdered by the Ripper, sent a message asking if I could give her a sitting.

There weren't many gaps in my diary at the time but I felt so sorry for that tragic family that I couldn't refuse.

We arrived in Chapeltown, a run down area of Leeds, on a dull, bleak day in early spring. The MacDonalds were just ordinary working people like John and I and they lived in a neat, square council house on an estate, separated from Chapeltown by a busy main road. Sadness seemed to hang over the house like low cloud and the plants in the wintry garden had a bedraggled, neglected look. They've lost heart, I thought, as I walked up the path and I hoped very much that I could help them.

Wilf MacDonald opened the door. He was a tall, thin man with receding silver hair. He seemed rather uneasy every time his glance met mine. I smiled at him encouragingly, thinking he might be nervous but he only looked away quickly.

'Look,' he said in the end as he took my coat, 'I've got to tell you. I've got no faith in what you do. I only agreed to go along with this because Irene wanted it. I don't believe in it at all.'

'That's all right,' I told him, glad he'd found the courage to speak his mind right away. 'What you believe is your privilege. I'll just get on with my work and you can make up your own mind.'

Hearing our voices Irene came out to meet us and I was immediately struck by the similarity between them. Irene was small while her husband was tall, pleasantly plump while Wilf was thin, and she had thick, springy dark hair while he was grey, but the same haunted look burned in both their eyes making them look like brother and sister.

Outwardly the strain showed more on Irene than on Wilf. Deep lines of suffering ran round her mouth, there were sleepless bags beneath her eyes and her hands clenched and unclenched as she spoke. With Wilf the pain lay under the surface. Irene told me that he'd suffered from nervous asthma since his daughter's murder and it was so bad he'd had to retire from his job on the railways five years early. He wasn't the man he used to be, she confided. Even little jobs around the house got too much for him at times.

Wilf went out to the kitchen to make a pot of tea and watching him go I realized that there's never just one victim of a murder. The effects of such a senseless, wicked act go on and on, spreading like ripples on a pond, ruining the lives of everyone involved.

A few minutes later Wilf came back, he and Irene drew their chairs close to mine and I tuned in. There was no trouble reaching Jayne. Her clear young voice piped up immediately and I felt she'd been trying to contact her parents for some time.

'Hello, I'm Jayne,' she said excitedly, glad to be talking to them at last.

'I'm Doris, love,' I said. 'Can you tell us what happened to you? Can you remember?'

'My daddy said I had to be in by eleven,' said Jayne slowly.

Wilf nearly shot out of his chair. 'That's right. I did,' he cried in amazement.

'But I missed the bus,' Jayne went on, 'so I walked home with my boyfriend. We thought his sister might give me a lift home but she was out so Steven walked part of the way with me and then I went on alone.'

Her voice seemed to trail off at the end of the sentence and in its place a picture flashed into my mind. I could see a patch of grass and a set of concrete steps. I stared at them, puzzled. They couldn't be described as a staircase – there weren't enough of them and they didn't lead anywhere. It was just a set of steps, left for some reason on a patch of grass. It made no sense at all. What a peculiar thing to show me, I thought.

'I'm sorry,' I said to the MacDonalds, 'I can't make anything of this but they're showing me a set of steps that don't lead anywhere.'

Irene and Wilf exchanged glances sharply. 'Yes, I know where that is,' was Irene's only comment.

Then I got a name: Sutcliffe.

'Sutcliffe was my maiden name,' Irene ventured.

'They're saying John Sutcliffe,' I said. 'Would that be your father?'

Irene shook her head. 'No – I think we might have had someone way back called John Sutcliffe. Is it him?'

But it wasn't. Instead I heard another woman's voice. She said she was Jayne's grandmother and Irene's mother. Her name was Annie. She talked for a while about members of the family and personal details and then she drew my attention back to the steps. They formed again in my mind. 'They are important,' Annie insisted.

'I don't understand why, Irene,' I said, 'but Annie is going on about the steps too. They are important for some reason.'

'I know what it means,' Irene admitted. 'Jayne's body was found in an adventure playground. The steps were built for the children to play on.'

There was a moment's silence then Jayne came back. 'I wish I'd rung Uncle Jack,' she said wistfully.

'Who's Uncle Jack, love?' I asked.

'Oh he's not our real uncle. We just call him Uncle,' Jayne explained. 'He lives over the back. He's a taxi driver. I wish I'd rung him to pick me up but I thought it was too late to wake him.'

'What happened after you left Steven, Jayne?' I asked. 'Can you tell us anything about the man who attacked you?'

'I didn't see him,' she explained. 'I heard these footsteps coming up behind me and then an arm went round my neck and my chain came off. I think he was wearing something dark, overalls or something like that. Then he hit me and I don't remember anything else.'

Irene didn't know what Jayne meant about the chain, but later she asked the girl who'd called for Jayne the night she was murdered if Jayne had been wearing a chain of any kind. 'Oh yes,' the girl had replied, 'she was wearing a crucifix round her neck.' Irene went up to check in Jayne's jewellery box and sure enough the crucifix was missing.

'What do you look like, Jayne?' I asked, realizing that I hadn't asked her to describe herself.

'I've got shoulder length brown hair with two blonde pieces at the front,' she explained.

At this information Wilf broke down. 'Yes, that's right,' he said. 'And when I went to identify her body, her head was bandaged and all I could see were these blonde bits covered in blood . . .'

Jayne couldn't bear to see her father's distress. For a

split second she materialized, a fresh pretty young girl with a glowing face and I saw her sit on the arm of her father's chair and lean towards him.

'Wilf, can you feel a pressure down one side?' I asked him. He looked up at me in surprise. 'Why, yes. As a matter of fact I can, and I feel warm all down here.' He waved his arm to indicate an area from his shoulder to his waist. 'How did you know?'

'Because Jayne's sitting on the side of your chair,' I explained. Wilf was speechless but his eyes met mine in wonder and for the rest of the sitting he kept staring at the empty air beside him as if willing Jayne to materialize.

By this time Jayne was getting tired with the effort of making her first communication. She mentioned a few more names including that of Paul Walker. Apparently after the tragedy Wilf could no longer manage some of the household chores he used to do and Paul Walker had come in to help with the tasks that were getting urgent.

Then the name John Sutcliffe came again, as it had come several times during the sitting.

'Well, I suppose one of your long lost relatives must be trying to get through, Irene,' I said, 'but he doesn't seem to be managing it. I haven't heard a man's voice at all.' She shrugged and it was only long afterwards that, by coincidence, we noticed that the man the police had arrested in connection with the murders was called Peter John Sutcliffe. However, the police assured Irene that he wasn't a distant relative.

At the end of the sitting Wilf went to fetch my coat and Irene told me a strange thing. Apparently the night Jayne died, Irene was out at her waitressing job and when she came home, tired because it was very late, she asked Wilf if all the children were back. He said they were, and that she could lock up.

'What about Jayne?' Irene had asked for some reason.

'Oh yes, she went up to bed a few minutes ago,' Wilf

had told her. So they locked the door and went to bed themselves.

The next morning when Wilf woke Irene with a cup of tea he looked worried.

'I can't understand it,' he said. 'I've just been into Jayne's room and she's not there and the bed hasn't been slept in. Yet I know she came in last night. I was dozing in the chair when she came in. She leaned over and kissed me goodnight. I saw her, heard her and smelled her perfume – but she's not there now.'

But as they discovered later, Jayne never did come home that night. By the time Wilf saw her she might already have been killed.

As we stood chatting in the hall ready to leave, someone said, 'Why don't we show Doris the stone steps she was on about? It's not far.'

'Well, if it won't upset Irene I don't mind,' I replied.

'No, I'm used to it by now,' Irene assured me, 'and you might get something else if you go there.' So we all piled into our waiting car and drove to the children's playground.

A damp spring breeze had come up while we were indoors and a few children were chasing each other round the jumble of play objects set out for them. The new grass was just coming through, there were tight buds on the trees and it was difficult to imagine that this place had been the scene of horror and brutality. But then Irene started combing the pavement for blood stains and the tragedy came flooding back.

'They found the blood out here but her body was in there,' Irene explained. 'She must have been dragged right through the playground.'

I looked across and there was the little flight of steps, just as I'd seen it in my mind earlier. I moved towards it and as I did so, I felt Jayne move in close to me again.

'Mum's never been to the grave,' she said. 'Don't go there, Mum, because I'm not there.'

I repeated this out loud to Irene. 'That's right,' she said.

'We've not been back since the day of the funeral. We couldn't face it.'

It had been a long emotional afternoon for the Mac-Donalds. They fell quiet as we walked around the play-ground and I know it was a strain for them.

'I'm getting tired. I can't work any more today,' I said after a while. 'Why don't we have another try tomorrow.' They agreed eagerly and I think we were all relieved to leave that sad place.

Wilf and Irene were silent most of the way home and I couldn't help wondering if we'd been any use to them. I needn't have worried. Later Irene phoned to say they'd been so overwhelmed they hadn't been able to take it all in, but afterwards they'd talked it over and even Wilf was impressed. It had made a tremendous difference to them. They even thought that if we carried on with our sittings, we might get some tiny clue, so far overlooked, which might help the police find Jayne's killer.

By this time I was feeling almost as involved as they were in the Ripper case. Having seen at first hand the suffering he caused I wanted to do everything I could to stop this man killing again and destroying another family, so I made arrangements to return to the MacDonald home for another sitting.

This time it was decided that the events should be recorded just in case there was something the police could use. A tape recorder was set up on the table in front of me where it would easily pick up my voice and a brand new cassette tape, fresh from its cellophane wrapper was inserted. Someone switched on the recorder to test it, while I was clearing my mind ready to tune in, and then suddenly, from the blank cassette we all heard someone speak.

'Hello,' said an excited girl's voice, followed by another word that was indistinct, then there was a burst of young laughter and then silence.

'That was Jayne!' cried Irene, her eyes shining and she

lunged towards the tape recorder where the cassette was spinning noiselessly, as if she thought Jayne might be hiding inside.

'Now hang on a minute, love,' I said cautiously. 'I know it sounded like a voice but it might have been a noise on the machine. A fault of some kind. Let's play it back and see if we still hear it.'

The tape was rewound and switched on again and Wilf and Irene craned eagerly over it. The little wheels turned silently for an age. The tension grew. We hardly dared breathe lest the noise should drown that brief sound and then, suddenly, there it was again. 'Hello—' the last word was lost in static, then came peals of girlish laughter and then nothing. Just blank tape.

'It's Jayne! I know it is. I'd know her voice anywhere,' Irene insisted. 'She said Hello, Mum! Play it again.'

Back went the tape to the beginning and we played it again and again and again. Irene was adamant that the message was 'Hello, Mum' but I wasn't sure. I never did catch that last word though there was no doubt that the first word was 'Hello'.

The MacDonalds were thrilled and would have sat there happily playing that fragment of tape until they wore it out, but I was still cautious.

'All right, it's definitely a voice,' I pointed out. 'But are you sure it's Jayne's voice? What did she sound like on a tape recorder? Have you got anything we can compare it with?'

Irene looked blank for a moment, then she jumped up. 'Of course we have. The girls were always playing about with the tape recorder. There'll be a tape upstairs.'

She hurried off, rummaged around upstairs and after a few minutes reappeared with a cassette. First we played the old recording and then the new. We tried them several times and I have to admit the voices sounded remarkably similar.

What with the excitement of the recording, we never did

get anything of use to the police on tape that day, but one interesting point stands out in my memory. When I finally contacted Jayne she said, 'Mum's been to the cemetery.' I thought I must have misheard because I distinctly remembered her saying on the last occasion we spoke that her parents had never been back to the grave.

'Sorry, Jayne,' I apologized, 'I thought you said your mother's been back to the cemetery.'

'Yes, that's right,' Jayne assured me, 'she has.'

Confused, I turned to Irene. Ramanov, my guide, had always taught me to check a message I was unsure of and if it came back as correct, then to repeat it aloud, however improbable it sounded.

'Well this sounds wrong to me, Irene,' I said, 'but Jayne tells me you've been back to the cemetery.'

Irene blushed. 'Yes, that's right, we have,' she said. 'You see, with all the other funeral expenses we hadn't been able to afford a headstone for the grave but the very same day we did the sitting, a reporter came and said that if we'd agree to be photographed by the grave, the paper would buy the stone for us. We'd felt so bad about Jayne having such a bare grave that we said yes.'

The MacDonalds were very pleased with the results, in fact Irene said I'd changed her life and Wilf admitted that he'd got his faith back. I was fired with enthusiasm to work on the Ripper case. So far, although I'd had very good contact with Jayne, we'd come up with frustratingly little in the way of tangible clues, but if we continued to work on it I felt we'd stumble across something useful.

I couldn't stay in Leeds, of course. I had the flat to look after and a stack of washing and ironing to do but I went home fully intending to carry on with the case from London.

Then one morning shortly after our return, John brought the papers in as usual. I'd finished the hoovering and washed up the breakfast things so I treated myself to a cup of coffee, a cigarette and a five minute read. I sat there with my feet up slowly turning the pages and shaking my head over the more horrifying stories. Then I turned a page and a large black headline leapt out at me: *Doris Stokes Victim*. I almost dropped the paper. Shocked, my hands shaking I read it again. *Doris Stokes Victim*. There was no mistake or coincidence. They were talking about me.

Carefully spreading the page on my knee so I wouldn't drop it, I read the story. Apparently my comments on the so called Yorkshire Ripper tape had been followed up and a man with the name Ronnie or Johnnie who lived in Berwick Street, Sunderland, and whose Sunderland accent matched the voice on the tape had been found. From time to time he even visited the places where the bodies had been found but he insisted he was innocent and the police believed him. However, he'd suffered a great deal of anxiety and suspicion because of me. So much so the paper had dubbed him my 'victim'.

I was absolutely aghast. All I'd tried to do was please the television people and help the police when I'd worked with that tape. I hadn't promised anything. I hadn't said that the Ronnie or Johnnie whose impression came from the voice was the Yorkshire Ripper, and I'd never suggested that this Sunderland man, a complete stranger to me, was the man I was referring to in connection with the tape. Yet, nevertheless, this man was suffering because of me.

I was terribly upset. All day guilt and regret nagged at me. I couldn't settle to anything. No matter what I started to do I somehow found myself back in front of the paper, staring at the photograph of that indignant man and his wife beneath the devastating headline. The words hurt afresh every time I read them. *Doris Stokes Victim*. I hadn't been given my gift for this. My job was to ease suffering not to cause it. With the best intentions in the world I'd failed Ramanov and misused my powers.

I remained in depression for hours and nothing John or Terry could say would console me. Then during the evening I heard Ramanov's voice gently reproving me for forgetting one of his earlier teachings. 'There is no point in brooding on past mistakes. What's past is past and cannot be changed. It is human to make errors. So learn from them, profit by them and go forward.'

Right, I thought. I will learn from it. From now on, no more Yorkshire Ripper work. I'll leave that case strictly to the police.

It wasn't long, however, before I came up against the double edged power of publicity once more.

Before I left for New York, Mike my American friend had telephoned and asked if I could possibly do anything by phone for a distraught lady who was right there with him in his office.

'Well I don't know, Mike,' I said. 'I'll try. You never can tell with phone contacts, sometimes they work, sometimes they don't.'

'She'd be very grateful if you could just try,' he assured me. There were some muffled clunks as he passed the receiver to someone else and the next minute a young woman's voice said, 'Hello, Doris. I'm Julie Patz.'

'Hello, Julie,' I replied and even as I spoke a strong impression of a child seemed to come to me across the three thousand miles of Atlantic that separated us. 'Julie,' I went on, 'I have a feeling this is about a child. A child who's gone missing.'

'Yes, that's right,' she gasped, her voice breaking. Then in the background I heard a man who spoke with a heavy European accent. 'I'm Hymie. Stanley's grandfather,' he said.

Julie explained that her husband's name was Stanley and his grandfather was known as Hymie. Hymie explained that the child, a little boy of six, had disappeared on his way to the school bus. He never did reach the bus. Tearfully Julie agreed that this was true.

'And I've got an unusual name here,' I went on, 'Aiden or Eiten or something like that.'

'Etan,' Julie corrected me. 'That's him. That's my son.'

Then the voice faded away and in my mind's eye I was walking up a street. Tall buildings towered on either side of me and I saw a shop with the words 'Mary's Candy Store' painted on the glass. Three doors along there was a laundrette filled with stacks of dirty washing and apartments over the top. Then the picture dissolved and as it faded out I heard someone say 'Ritchie'.

Then I was back in our hall again. Quickly I described the scene to Julie.

'Oh, I know that street,' she said. 'We often took Etan to Mary's to buy candy.'

'That's where he disappeared from,' I explained to her. 'He went from that street.'

The picture appeared to signal the end of the communication. Hymie had gone and nothing else came.

'Never mind, Julie,' I said, 'John and I are coming to New York soon. Perhaps Mike can bring us to see you and we'll try again.'

Naturally I didn't forget the case of little Etan Patz. Julie wrote to thank me for my work over the phone and in her letter she enclosed a picture of her missing son. He was such a beautiful child, I could have wept for his parents. With his big blue eyes, silky blond hair and friendly, wide-awake expression he looked like a child model. I put his picture on my shelf with all the other photographs of spirit children that parents had given me to look after. Not that anyone had told me Etan was on the other side, and I wouldn't have dreamed of saying so to Julie, but privately I thought the Patzes were unlikely to find their son alive.

As I looked at my little gallery of fresh young faces, I couldn't help thinking that it always seemed to be the brightest and most beautiful who pass over young. Why that should be I don't know. It doesn't seem fair – not to the people who love them, at any rate. Or perhaps they are specially privileged to care for such lovely little ones for the short time they have to complete on earth.

I often think that about the parents of handicapped children. It's frequently the case that the parents of such children are the nicest, kindest, most loving of people and one finds oneself feeling especially sad that they are the ones whose children are handicapped. Yet now I wonder whether that is the very reason they have been chosen to undertake the difficult task — because they are special people. Anyone less special wouldn't be able to cope.

So when we arrived in New York the Patzes were among the first people we contacted. Julie invited us to visit them in Greenwich village. They had a vast, airy studio flat, open-plan style with the sitting-room created in a wall-less space by the clever arrangement of sofas, chairs and little tables.

Julie had made a pot of delicious, American coffee — a welcome change from the instant stuff John and I drink at home. We chatted while we drank and then I started to work. Hymie came back to talk to me again and told me about the fateful morning Etan went missing.

'He tells me you had another child in the house that morning,' I said.

'Yes,' said Julie. 'I've got two other children.'

'No, not one of yours. Another child.'

Julie looked blank.

'She doesn't know what you're talking about, Hymie,' I told him. 'Can you give us more information?' Back came the reply: Elizabeth.

'Who's Elizabeth?' I asked.

'Oh god, of course,' said Julie. 'I was looking after Elizabeth's baby, that's why I didn't take Etan to the bus like I usually do.'

Hymie mentioned more family details and then I heard a different, young voice. He didn't give me his name and the communication was faint and difficult. It might have been Etan but I couldn't be certain since he didn't tell me his name and so could have been another child connected with the family. Of course I didn't want to upset the Patzes unnecessarily if there was still a slim chance that Etan was alive. The boy, whoever he was, kept talking about a special cap and he went on and on about it as if it was important.

'I know what he means,' said Julie. 'Etan was crazy about baseball and we bought him a cap in a sale which used to belong to a real baseball player. Etan thought the world of that cap. He wore it all the time, even to school.'

The boy went on to tell me many names of people Etan used to go and see. The list made me uneasy: they were all names of men and the child was only six years old.

By the end of the sitting Julie had collected a mass of family information and several bits and pieces about the day Etan disappeared, but of Etan's present whereabouts, there was not a clue. Unless we'd been given a hint but had failed to recognize the information for what it was. I've often found in the past that it's only when a case has been solved and the whole story is revealed that one realizes that a solid clue had been staring one in the face all along.

Julie was pleased with what we'd got so far but naturally disappointed that we hadn't managed to locate Etan. There was still a lot of work to do on the case. I had a feeling it was going to be a complicated story and I promised Julie I'd work with Etan's photograph whenever I had time.

Over the next few days John and I were rushed hither and thither to be interviewed by this person, to do a sitting for that person, a phone-in for someone else until we hardly knew what day of the week it was. At one point, someone who had heard about my sitting with Julie Patz and the reference to Mary's Candy Store asked if I would agree to be filmed outside the shop to see if I could get any more information from being on the spot. It's sometimes very successful to go to the scene, so I asked, 'Does Julie know about this?'

'Oh yes,' I was assured. 'She thinks it's a great idea.' So I agreed.

94

A car was sent to fetch us and we drove through a maze of anonymous streets from our hotel until suddenly we turned a corner and I had a strange feeling of *déjà vu*. This was the street Hymie had shown me. I knew it without recognizing anything. The next second Mary's Candy Store came into view. It was like watching a dream turn into reality. The car pulled up outside and I could see the film unit arriving but there was no sign of Julie.

'I wonder where she's got to?' I said to John.

'She'll probably be here in a minute,' John replied. 'It looks as if we're early. They're not ready for us yet.'

We wanted to take some tonic water back to the hotel with us so while we waited we popped into Mary's Candy Store. There was a woman and a little boy behind the counter and as she served me the woman was peering hard at my face.

'Haven't I seen you somewhere before?' she asked.

'I don't think so,' I said, 'unless you've seen me on television.'

She looked quizzical, so I explained I was a medium and that I was visiting the area to see if I could help in the Etan Patz case.

'Oh yes, isn't it a shame about that little boy?' she agreed. She wrapped the tonic water and as she put it into my hand, something made me say, on impulse, 'Do you know someone called Ritchie who lives in the apartments above the laundry?'

'Yes,' she said. 'I know two Richies up there. Which one did you mean?'

Staggered, I could only say, 'Oh, I don't know.'

She looked at me curiously, then she bent and whispered something to the little boy who turned and ran off. We talked for a little longer and then as we left the shop we were surprised to see quite a number of Italians coming out of the apartment building. As they moved up the street everyone scattered and for a few moments, apart from the television crew, the place looked deserted.

'Well, that's odd!' I said to John. 'I wonder what that was all about.'

But there wasn't time to speculate. A reporter came over and started to interview me. I had to explain all over again how I'd become involved in the Etan Patz case and what information I'd come up with so far. The cameras had been rolling for several minutes when out of the corner of my eye I noticed a commotion going on. Turning my head slightly I could see that Julie had arrived and she was having a furious row with someone.

Uncomfortably aware there was something wrong, I lost track of what I was saying and my voice trailed away. Seeing that my attention had gone the reporter brought the interview to a premature close and I was able to hurry over to Julie.

'Oh, Doris, I know it's not your fault!' she cried.

'What isn't?' I asked bewildered. 'What's the matter?'

'All this!' she said angrily, waving her arm at the cameras and the newspapermen. 'Look at them! They didn't tell me you were doing this.'

'But they said you knew! They said you thought it was a good idea. I expected you to be here.'

'They didn't tell me a thing,' said Julie. 'I only found out by accident. I think it's dreadful. My son's missing and they're turning it into a circus!'

I was mortified. I put my arms around her. 'Oh, Julie, I'm so sorry. I had no idea you felt like that. I only did it because I thought you'd agreed.'

'Well, I didn't. I think it's disgusting.' And she began to sob, half in sorrow, half in anger. I felt like doing the same myself. The television crew melted tactfully, or possibly fearfully, away and we were left to comfort Julie as best we could. It was no use. Julie was sickened by the whole thing and wanted no more to do with mediums. For me the Etan Patz case was closed. I was very, very sad about it. Once more, publicity had turned my work sour.

Yet what was I to do? Through the press I was able to

reach thousands and thousands of people with the truth that there is no death, and for every painful disappointment like the Patzes and the Yorkshire Ripper case there were a hundred wonderful successes. I knew that, whatever the cost, I would have to go on, but that in future I would have to be far more cautious and far less trusting.

The only good thing I can say about the whole bitter lesson is that throughout it all I remained friends with Irene MacDonald. Poor Wilf never did get over Jayne's murder. His health declined steadily and he died suddenly. This time Irene knew just where to turn. She contacted me and I was able to do a sitting for her. Wilf came through very easily and among the things he mentioned was the fact that Irene had had a fire in her kitchen recently and he was very concerned.

'Tell her to be more careful in future,' he said. 'It was only sheer luck it wasn't a disaster.'

Irene was amazed. 'That's right,' she said. 'I'd left a large cardboard box on the sink next to the stove and it caught fire. By the time I got there it was flaming, but I just managed to get hold of it and throw it out of the door.'

I was a little puzzled because Wilf also kept referring to a pullover. 'Will you take this pullover off?' he kept repeating. When I mentioned it to Irene she was thrilled. 'Those were his last words!' she explained. Apparently she had bought him a pullover in a jumble sale and he hadn't liked it. Just before he collapsed he had decided he couldn't tolerate it any longer and had insisted Irene took it off him.

Wilf also told me joyfully that he'd met Jayne again and they were very happy. But they were worried about Irene. 'She takes too much valium,' said Wilf.

Irene promised to try to cut down as much as possible. 'I'm getting back to normal gradually,' she said bravely.

Looking back over the two cases I have mixed feelings. As far as I know, I've failed to help the police find the Ripper or Etan Patz. On the other hand, I've given the

MacDonalds and the Patzes a lot of information, food for thought and, in the case of Irene at least, comfort. In the end that's what my job is all about. I've never claimed to be a psychic detective. My gift was not given to me for that purpose. As Ramanov has often told me, we are here on earth to learn and we must solve our own problems. If the spirit world solved them for us we would learn nothing. But just occasionally, the victim of a murder is so angry about the crime that he is determined to come back and help bring his killer to justice. Sometimes, too, the murderer is known personally to the victim and there are often successful results, but of course, although the police can be told the identity of the killer, there is still no guarantee that the criminal will be caught. If there is no material evidence the police can do nothing.

So, frustrating though it is at times, I have to accept that if I can give comfort to the victim's family, I've done my job and anything more is an unexpected bonus.

I'll let Irene MacDonald have the last word on the subject:

'The last time I saw Jayne she was getting ready to go to her Saturday job. I know I'm her mother, but honestly she was such a pretty girl and so nice. She was always cheerful and smiling. Anyway, she said goodbye and she skipped off down the road, her whole life in front of her – and I never saw her again. The next thing I knew, she was dead.

'It's one of those things you always think happens to other people. You can't believe it can happen to you, and then it does. You can't absorb it somehow. I still find it hard to sleep and I'm on valium; Wilf couldn't take it at all.

'Everyone was shocked when they heard. I mean everyone loved Jayne. She was very fond of children and one little girl of twelve not far from us came home from school and fainted. They couldn't think what was wrong with her but it turned out she'd just heard about Jayne.

'It was awful the way up till then the others that were murdered were prostitutes. People who didn't know Jayne might have thought she was like that too, but she wasn't. She was still a virgin. We were a close family and we talked about it. Jayne used to say "No mum, I'll wait till I'm about nineteen and I've found the man I want to marry," and she meant it.

'Wilf and I both lost our religious faith and we were sceptical about Doris at first. We thought she'd be one of these posh television people but she wasn't like that at all.

'It was marvellous the things she told us. Little things she couldn't possibly have known, like the bit about our dog. She said she could hear a dog barking and Jayne told her she'd found our dog, whose name was Sam or Sammy. Well, he got called both those names. She even knew how the dog died, he was knocked down and the worst injuries were on his back legs. Jayne said she'd found the dog and his back legs were all right now.

'There's no explanation for things like that and it had a big effect on Wilf and I. Wilf used to say he'd got his faith back and he were a changed man, much more cheerful.

'The family's still not right, of course. If an ambulance goes down the road they look all round and then say, "Well, we're all here, it's not one of us," and when they walk in the door they see if everything's all right before they relax. My son Ian who's sixteen doesn't like to leave me, even to go to school. "What do you do when I've gone?" he keeps asking and when we go out together he stays by my side.

'Most of all we miss Wilf but thanks to Doris we know we shall see him again one day. I'm very glad we saw her when we did because as Wilf told one reporter shortly afterwards, "I'm not afraid to die any more because of Jayne — because I know she's there." '

CHAPTER 7

Looking back over the last few chapters it must sound as if my work is all misery and suffering, an endless procession of murders, tragic deaths and grieving families. Of course, those sort of cases do form the bulk of my work, but there are also light-hearted moments and we mediums enjoy a bit of fun as much as everyone else. Sometimes the spirit messages themselves are funny, sometimes it's the colourful characters of the church officials and sometimes I get myself into hilarious scrapes.

I'll never forget one meeting I did at a church where the president's wife, Vera, was also the secretary, treasurer and harmonium player. Vera was a short, plump little person and like me, very broad in the beam. She was also very fond of her little dog which she took everywhere with her, including the platform during meetings.

I was a little apprehensive about this as I thought the animal might get restless and unhappy, but in the event he behaved beautifully. Throughout the service he curled up on a chair and went to sleep. Then when Vera got up to play the last hymn the dog suddenly woke up, jumped off his seat and sprang onto the long organ stool beside her. Vera, who was already crashing out the opening bars, didn't appear to notice. She bashed away happily, lost in the music, swaying her plump body to the rhythm.

From round the hall under cover of the singing I heard a few titters. What was going on? I looked round and saw nothing unusual on the floor but as the hymn went on the laughter increased.

Puzzled, I stared at the strange little couple on the organ stool, side by side, Vera swaying, the dog wagging its tail, and then I noticed it. Every time Vera swayed to the left, the dog's tail wagged to the right and slapped her ample bottom. And so it went on, sway, slap, sway, slap, until I thought I'd have to stuff a handkerchief into my mouth to stop myself from laughing!

There was another lady, president of a church, who did a lot of good works. She had a ginger cat which used to sleep on top of the fridge in her kitchen, presumably because it was the warmest spot. This lady only had to start singing her favourite hymn, *I need thee, every hour I need thee*, in her not over-tuneful voice and the cat would leap off the fridge onto her lap and start licking her frantically all over the face. We never could work out whether he liked her singing or whether he was trying to get her to stop!

There are quite a few people who put on a 'platform' voice whenever they have to speak in public. It's probably nerves that causes it, but put them in front of more than six people and their normal speaking voice drops away and from nowhere comes a posh, slightly pompous tone, grappling with longer words than they would normally use.

Now this particular lady, who wasn't a bit pretentious or pompous, unfortunately fell into the 'platform' voice habit. Every time I listened to her on a stage, I marvelled at how much her voice could change and how she seemed totally unaware of the fact.

One evening we were doing a service together and the people who looked after the hall had decked the place with flowers and in front of the platform was the most beautiful arrangement of freesias, one of my favourite blooms. Throughout the service the wonderful perfume wafted up to us until we were drenched in it. My friend Rosemary was in the audience and every now and then I looked at her and smiled. Then at the end of the service the president stepped forward to thank everyone for a splendid effort.

I'd only been talking to her half an hour before and she'd sounded quite normal, but now out came this extraordinary voice. In plummy, but mangled tones she congratulated the women who'd made the hall look so nice. In front of me Rosemary's eyebrows rose quarter of an inch. I smiled and looked down.

'. . . And these *love—ly* flowers,' the president was trilling, 'all these fresians marching across the rostrum . . .'

Instantly, a picture of black and white cows trotting over the stage flashed before my eyes and I had to bite my lip very hard. I stole a glance at Rosemary. She was crimson in the face, her shoulders were shaking silently and she caught my eye. That did it. I just exploded and had to press a handkerchief over my mouth to change the giggles into a fit of coughing.

I did manage to do a bit of serious work though. A young girl who used to live in a high rise block of flats came through. She had fallen over a balcony and been killed and everyone had thought it was suicide. It was true she had been depressed, but she came back to tell them that her death was an accident.

'I was in a temper, I stormed out onto the balcony and the sheer force took me straight over the top,' she said. 'It happened so fast I hardly knew what was happening. One minute I was flouncing out of the french doors, the next I was in mid-air.' She mentioned a few more family details to her sister who was in the audience, and then she said cheekily, 'I see my new handbag matches your coat!'

The sister started to laugh with tears running down her face. 'Yes it does,' she said. 'As a matter of fact, I bought the coat to match the bag, because the bag was my sister's.'

The messages often make the sitter laugh. One of the strangest I ever received was for a woman who was introduced to me as 'Bubbles'. She was a widow and her husband came through and explained that her real name was Kathleen, but she was nicknamed Bubbles. As he talked, I could hear a strange screeching, squawking noise going on in the background and as soon as I got the chance I had to interrupt to ask what it was.

'Oh that. That's the parrot,' he said. 'Tell Kathleen I've got the parrot with me.'

I'd come across dogs and cats in the spirit world but never parrots. Anyway, I mentioned it to Bubbles.

'Oh yes,' she said, 'it used to belong to my mother and when she passed over we took it in.'

Her husband was quiet for a few moments and in the silence I distinctly heard the parrot cackle, 'Old Treacle-belly! Squawk, squawk. Old Treaclebelly!' I could hardly believe my ears, but there it was again, 'Old Treaclebelly!' I couldn't help laughing.

'What's the matter?' asked Bubbles.

'Well, quite honestly,' I said, 'I don't know whether you'll be annoyed or upset about this, but I'm certain I can hear the parrot saying Old Treaclebelly.'

And she burst out laughing. 'You couldn't have given me better proof, Doris,' she cried. 'When I was pregnant I had a thing about golden syrup. I ate golden syrup with everything. I was always eating it and my husband taught the parrot to say Old Treaclebelly!'

On another occasion I was speaking at a public meeting in Grantham when the president's husband came through. He described his wife's sitting room and the big stone fireplace which was the centre piece. As he spoke, a picture of the room came into my mind and at the end of the mantelpiece I could see a pair of false teeth, just sitting there all alone, grinning blankly into the room.

Of course, without thinking, I repeated aloud what I could see and the audience roared with laughter. Fortunately the president wasn't embarrassed.

'Yes, I used to get so annoyed with him,' she said. 'After he'd had a meal he'd sit down in the armchair, take out his false teeth and put them on the mantelpiece instead of taking them to the bathroom. But I couldn't change him. He always did it.'

Strangely enough you often come across mention of teeth in spirit messages. I remember being in contact with an old lady who'd passed with a cerebral haemorrhage. She chatted away eagerly but her speech was a little blurred and indistinct. Once or twice I had to ask her to repeat a sentence and in the end she said, 'Can't you understand what I say, dear? You see they sent me over without my teeth.' Apparently, after she'd had the stroke they had removed her false teeth to avoid injury and hadn't put them back again. Her guide must have forgotten to explain how to get them back.

'Just think your own natural teeth back and they'll come,' I advised her.

'Are you sure, dear?' she asked.

'Well, that's what I've been told,' I said.

There was a silence filled with deep concentration and then suddenly she was back, clear and precise with no slurring, 'You're right!' she said. 'They've all come back. The full set.'

She was thrilled and thought I was immensely clever but of course it was nothing like that: I was only repeating what Ramanov had told me. I have no idea how it works.

Generally it seems that when a person passes, his appearance returns to that which he had when he was last healthy and strong. If he lost his hair or teeth prematurely he can restore them if he wishes simply by 'thinking' them back. Disabilities and handicaps seem to be corrected automatically. A thalidomide child, for instance, would immediately become whole and perfect, the way he should have been born had nothing gone wrong.

This was proved to me during a sitting in Liverpool. A little boy, no more than 5 years old, came back to talk to his grandma. He spoke perfectly and answered a lot of questions without hesitation but when I asked him his name, he began to stutter.

'Mar, mar, mar, mar . . .' he kept repeating as if he was trying to say Mark. I couldn't understand this because every other word had been pronounced properly. Surely his name would be easiest of all? Remembering Ramanov's rule, however, I said aloud exactly what I was hearing and the grandmother gasped.

'That's it,' she cried. 'That's exactly the way he used to say it. He was mentally handicapped you see and couldn't speak properly.'

Little Mark was no longer mentally handicapped and he could now speak as well as anyone, but he'd used his old pronunciation of his name to prove to his grandmother it was really him.

Sometimes incidents are only funny in retrospect and these little adventures tend to happen when I'm dashing about from place to place trying to fit far too much into too short a time.

Once I was asked to conduct a service at St Anne's church near Blackpool. The people who ran the church were old friends and I didn't want to disappoint them, but unfortunately I had another engagement the day before and I didn't see how I could reach St Anne's on time. Then Terry came to the rescue.

'Why don't you fly?' he suggested. Terry had always been interested in machines of all kinds. He learned to drive a car as soon as he was legally allowed and now he belonged to a flying club. His greatest dream was to get his pilot's licence.

'But you haven't got your licence yet,' I reminded him.

'It doesn't matter,' he said confidently. 'One of the lads will run you up in no time.'

Though John and I weren't very keen on flying, we did want to get to St Anne's, so we agreed and set off on the appropriate day with Judy, an old friend, for Biggin Hill aerodrome.

'Have you ever flown before?' asked one of the ground crew as we hurried through the gate.

'Oh, yes,' I said more confidently than I felt. 'We've been to the Isle of Man.'

He led us across the tarmac, threading our way between all kinds of impressive machines in an astonishing assortment of shapes and colours, and then unexpectedly the man stopped.

'There you are. That's yours,' he said, pointing at one of the tiniest planes I'd ever seen. It looked as fragile as a dragon-fly. I was just about to protest that there must be some mistake, we couldn't possibly be flying all the way to Blackpool in that, when I noticed Terry and another young man checking the instruments.

Oh, my God, I thought.

'Come on then!' shouted Terry, sticking his head out of the miniature door. 'What are you waiting for? I thought you were in a hurry?'

'It's a bit small, isn't it?' I muttered nervously.

'Nonsense,' said Terry. 'You don't need a jumbo jet for five of us.'

So we gingerly climbed aboard – at least the others did; they had to haul me up since I'm not built for climbing – and we squeezed into the doll size passenger compartment.

'Don't be alarmed if we hit a few bumps,' the pilot told us cheerfully when we were strapped into our seats. 'I haven't flown one of these before.'

I should have got out then, I suppose, but Terry slammed the door, the engines roared, we lurched off down the runway and lunged clumsily into the sky.

I need hardly add that it was a terrible flight. The little plane hit every air pocket it could find as if bent on suicide. We bounced and rocked all over the sky, dipping and soaring with vibrations fit to tear the cabin apart. The clouds went up and down outside the portholes like waves around a ship and even Judy, a New Zealand girl and a hardened traveller, went green in the face.

The noise was deafening but over the top we could hear the pilot cursing at Terry who was navigating. Towards the end of the flight he was yelling at the top of his voice.

'Well, I'm sorry,' Terry yelled back over the screaming engines 'but I'm navigating properly.'

And then the pilot suddenly clapped one hand to his

forehead. 'Oh my god, Terry. I've been reading the wrong instruments!'

If John, Judy and I had had parachutes I think we would have bailed out then. As it was, we shut our eyes and prayed. Fortunately God was looking after us and by some miracle we landed at Squires Gate airstrip in one piece.

I was feeling dreadful. My head was swimming, my ears roaring and the floor was still going up and down under my feet. Dimly I was aware that John and Judy had scrambled out and Terry was squeezing back to give me a hand. He led me to the doorway and pointed out a tiny little steel foot-rest just below the lip of the opening.

'Put your foot on that and jump,' he shouted in my ear.

I looked at the tarmac a long way down and, as I watched, it rushed up to meet me and then fell dizzily away again.

'There's no way I can jump,' I shouted back and then I noticed that just beside the door was the base of the wing which sloped gently down almost to the ground. 'I'll get down my way,' I said and before he had time to stop me, I clambered out, perched myself on the wing and slid down. As I whistled towards the ground, my skirt up, my stockings ripping and tearing, I saw the reception committee lined up on the tarmac to meet me and in the front row were the photographers, cameras clicking, recording every second for posterity!

The meeting was worth all the trouble, however. People from miles around packed into the hall and the messages came through with unusual vigour as if my hair-raising journey had somehow strengthened the contact. Perhaps I'd been closer to the spirit world than I'd realized!

One man boldly said he wanted to speak to Nancy from Lytham. He was her husband, he explained, and he'd cut his throat. How can I say that in public, I thought, but the man insisted he wanted to say hello to his wife and the light remained firmly over a pale woman in the middle of the hall.

'Are you Nancy?' I asked looking directly at her.

'Oh. Yes,' she gasped.

'I've got your husband here,' I said. 'He went over very quickly. *Very quickly indeed*,' I stressed.

The woman nodded. 'Yes. That's right.'

'You can tell them I cut my throat,' the man interrupted. 'And my poor wife found me.'

'I can't say that out loud,' I protested.

'Yes you can,' he said and the impression was so vivid I found myself looking at a big double bed, the white sheets all red with blood.

Helplessly, I drew my hand across my own throat. I didn't say anything, I just looked at the woman. She knew what I meant.

'Yes, that's right,' she whispered.

Her husband went on to say that she had moved and was living at a new address and that she had just come back from America. Both facts were correct.

The meeting went on quite successfully for some time and then a lady in the front row stood up. I didn't have any message for her but she said, 'I would like to say something, if I might.'

'Yes, dear, that's all right with me,' I said tolerantly but my heart began to race fearing she was going to complain about something or try to pick a quarrel.

'I'd just like to make this declaration,' she said and then I noticed she was looking past me and in her hand was a white stick. Bless her heart, she's blind, I thought, ashamed.

'Two years ago I went to Lancaster to see Doris Stokes for a sitting,' the woman continued, oblivious of my turmoil. 'She told me I would marry and that my name would be Armstrong. I went away quite convinced she was a fake because I couldn't imagine how on earth I was going to meet a man who would be willing to marry me with my disability. But ladies and gentlemen, I would now like to introduce you to my husband whose name is Mr Armstrong!' The tall pleasant looking man beside her stood up and bowed awkwardly to the audience and the whole place exploded into cheers and clapping. It was a marvellous way to end a marvellous meeting.

We stayed three days with our friends in the North. I told Terry I'd go back by train, but he insisted our problems were due entirely to the size of the plane and promised to return with a larger model. Somehow I let myself be talked into flying again, but Terry was as good as his word. He returned with a chunky, solid-looking machine and the flight was smooth and without incident. Only one person was alarmed. A reporter from the *Psychic News* flew with us to interview me about the meeting at St Anne's. Checking through his notebook he said idly, 'I wonder where we are now.'

'Half a minute, I'll ask Head Office,' I joked but I enquired anyway, and back came a voice saying Birmingham. 'We're at Birmingham,' I told him.

'Oh,' he said indulgently, continuing with his notes, and then suddenly over the intercom came the pilot's voice:

'We are now passing over Birmingham.'

The reporter dropped his notebook like a hot coal and shifted back in his seat to increase the distance between us. For the rest of the flight he regarded me warily and I think he would have been much happier continuing his journey by train!

I do sometimes forget that some people are easily alarmed and I tend to speak without thinking. I remember when I was packing to leave for Australia last time, Matey was driving me mad. He was circling the flat making a dreadful row and nothing I could do would stop him. I gave him food, milk, water and a cuddle but still he cried and howled. My nerves were on edge in any case about the coming trip and the long flight and I thought if he carried on much longer I would scream.

'What's the matter with the cat?' I asked the spirit world in desperation.

Back came the answer, 'He's got toothache.'

Relieved, I phoned the vet and explained to the helpful receptionist what was wrong.

'That's all right, Mrs Stokes, the vet will be round soon,' she said. 'But how do you know your cat's got toothache?'

'The spirit people told me,' I said thoughtlessly.

There was a pause. 'I beg your pardon?' she said.

Oh, well, I've done it now, I thought. 'The spirit people,' I repeated boldly.

There was a long silence. 'Are you still there?' I asked.

'Eh, yes, yes, Mrs Stokes,' the girl said faintly. 'The vet will be right round,' and she put the phone down.

The vet, however, was made of sterner stuff.

'So you're the lady who talks to spirits,' he said cheerfully as he came into the flat.

'Yes, that's right,' I told him. 'And they've just told me your name is Peter.'

He almost dropped his bag. 'Why, yes, it is. How did you know?' He saw my smile. 'Oh yes, sorry. The spirit people!'

And when he examined Matey he discovered the spirit people had been right about that, too. Matey was indeed suffering from toothache.

CHAPTER 8

'Now then, Doris, just look into my eyes . . . I want you to listen to my voice . . . you are getting heavier and heavier. Every muscle in your body is loose and heavy . . . you are sinking . . . sinking . . .'

An overpowering drowsiness was stealing over me: my arms and legs felt so heavy that they would melt through the couch; my head sank on my chest; my eyelids began to droop and a long way off, someone was saying, 'Listen to my voice . . .'

Some strange things have happened to me in the past but one of the strangest was certainly my hypnotic regression. While I was still in New York, Dick Sommers who had invited me onto his radio show, asked if I would like to undergo hypnotic regression.

Dick, a very suave young man with piercing dark eyes, was interested in all types of psychic phenomena and he was also an accomplished hypnotist. He explained that under hypnotic trance some people seem able to recall 'past lives' in astonishing detail. Whether this was evidence of reincarnation or simply the brain's ability to store apparently forgotten facts picked up over the years and present them in story form almost like dreams, no one knows but according to Dick quite uneducated people appear to have greater knowledge of life hundreds of years ago than historians who have spent decades studying the subject.

I don't have any firm views on reincarnation myself. I know that occasionally people seem to 'disappear' from the spirit world. You might be in regular contact with them over the years and then suddenly, for no apparent reason, they don't come back any more. Whether they have progressed to a higher plane or whether they have come back to earth in another body, I couldn't say, although Ramanov did mention once that if we didn't learn the lesson we were sent here to learn the first time, we'd only have to come back and do it again, which does seem to indicate some form of reincarnation.

Anyway, I explained to Dick that I found the whole subject confusing but I was quite willing to try the experiment if he was.

So on a crisp morning in spring, John and I presented ourselves at Dick's plush office high up in a skyscraper next to the UN Building. Looking out of the picture windows made me feel dizzy but apart from that the office was extremely comfortable. There were big, green, jungly plants everywhere and soft brown furnishings. John sat down on the sofa, but Dick put me in a big leather armchair, pressed a button and it went back just like a dentist's chair.

'Now there is nothing to worry about, Doris,' he said. 'You just relax, listen to my voice and you'll feel as if you're asleep.'

All the same I found it difficult to relax completely. Although I'd agreed to the experiment, I wasn't completely happy about it. I knew that under hypnosis I wouldn't be in control of myself and that was an uncomfortable feeling . . . but Dick was telling me to look into his eyes and as I stared into bottomless brown, and listened to his velvet voice, my mind drifted away and I fell asleep.

I have no recollection of what happened next. Dimly I was aware of someone saying, 'listen to my voice . . .' from time to time and once or twice something brushed my face, but apart from that it was as if I was in a deep, dreamless sleep. Dick recorded the session, however, and this is a transcript of what I said:

DICK: *You're going back, back, back . . . Now, where are you, Doris?*

DORIS(distressed): *We have to fight . . . we have to fight. Please*

When I told Janet of A M America that I didn't tell fortunes, she couldn't understand what I would do.

Meet my family of spirit children. Pictured here are: Thomas Oliver, Biancha, Dr David Court, Peter, John Michael, Lidga, John Pigeon, Linda, Etan, Gregg, Robert,

Stephen, Carreen, Charmian, Richard and Jenny.
(Photo: Michael Dearsley)

After the publication of VOICES IN MY EAR we received so much mail, the whole family had to help.

Here I am on the Late Late Show in Dublin.

The highlight of my visit to New Zealand was the Maori welcome at Rotorua Airport, but I felt so sorry for the Maoris shivering in the cold.

'We love Granny Doris' the children from Rotorua wrote in the steam on the windows.

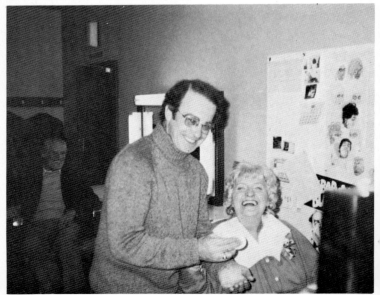

Here I am getting made up for the Roger Mahoney show.

**Yolande Finch came for a sitting and soon I was having a
very frank talk with the famous film star, Peter Finch.**
(Photo: Michael Dearsley)

Daniel was telling me about his funeral and he kept drawing a machine in the air. 'It was made of flowers,' he said. What on earth could it be?

don't let them catch us . . . Where are the voices? Why have you deserted? Where are my voices? You held the cross for me through the smoke. I did not betray my voices . . . St Catherine give me strength, I will not betray my voices . . .

DICK: *Where are you, Doris? What year is it?*

DORIS: *I am in Paris. It's seventeen-sixty-something. My name is Joan. I'm just a farmer's daughter . . . The farm is in the country but I had to go to Paris because my . . . France . . . Charles has been ravaged . . . I know that my voices are truthful. My voices have deserted me, maybe they are right, maybe I'm mad. I know God is on my side. God will look after me. We must fight. We must save France. Are you Pierre?*

DICK: *Who's Pierre?*

DORIS: *He was the man I was going to marry. I had to leave him because the voice told me to. It said I must go and offer myself for service.*

DICK: *What voice, Doris?*

DORIS: *It was St Catherine, she told me. It was St Catherine, she told me in my ear when I was doing the cattle. She said I must go and fight. They laughed at me, a peasant girl, going to court but I did and we fought and we won and when they saw that good was triumphing over evil they took me away . . . God, I can see him. He said it was in the name of God . . . always blood-red he wore, the colour of blood. I was very lonely, they wouldn't let me talk or see anyone . . . All he said was repent, repent . . . all the blood he shed. He was a cardinal; I wish I could remember his name.*

It's 1763 . . . so cold . . . I'm in a cart, wooden wheels and cobbled streets, it throws me from side to side but I have not gone back on my voices . . . whatever is to come I will stand firm. Why are the people jeering at me? (voice breaking in distress) *Do you not know it was for you? Why do you have to rope me like an animal? Oh, the voices, do not desert me now! Dear God, do not desert me now! I know what is ahead of me now. Let it be quick.*

DICK (trying to calm things): *Now we are going back to when you were a little girl. Tell me what you can see.*

DORIS: *Mmmmmmum makes the butter; sometimes I turn the*

113

handle. *I'm so small it lifts me off my feet when I turn the churn with my mum. Grandmère also. We work. Grandmère is very good with needles; she makes not a lot of money. Always we had a little white cap and collar. I am at the farm. I am five; I have two brothers, they are older, François and André. They tease me. We gather apples. Martine is my cousin, she is coming for my birthday tomorrow . . . Tomorrow I will be seven. Martine thinks she's very grand because she lives in the city but my hair is just as pretty. I have brown hair, lots of brown hair . . . but they cut it all off . . . when I was a soldier I could not go to war and fight so I cut it off, but they shaved me . . . those men . . . . in the name of religion, they did it . . . I am eighteen.*

DICK: *When did you hear the voices?*

DORIS: *When Martine came I first heard the voice. We'd been to pray, there was a shrine on the hill to our blessed Mary and we'd been to place flowers and I heard the voice that said she was St Catherine and Martine she laughed at me but I did not say. It was my secret. The voices I heard were my voices . . . several voices but St Catherine was the only one I talked directly to . . . We need more horses . . . We have camped outside the city walls. The walls are high, we must scale the walls, Jan. Jan he has made me a sword. Some soldiers laugh at me, they say they will not follow a girl but I know my voices tell me, 'Lead them, Joan. Lead them.' And I did, not for glory, I didn't do it for that but because I loved France . . .*

(sobbing) *Dear God make it quick . . . The smoke! The smoke! I don't mind the pain, the smoke! I can't breathe! I can't breathe! Please God, make me unconscious. Reach my chest! Let me see the cross! Death is sweet . . .*

(calm again)*I am home. Dear St Catherine, I did not fail you. I did not fail you. Forgive me for being weak for a while but I did not fail you. It is over. It is in God's hands now . . . Our beloved country. He is just a painted doll and he has our country at his mercy . . .*

DICK: *Tell me about heaven.*

DORIS: *Aaaahhhh such magnificence, such flowers, deep blue . . .*

*To see the lakes . . . such beauty . . . But I have been to earth
again that is why I'm so confused . . .*

(voice changes, becoming flirtatious. A French accent)

*I am Odette. I have been to Rome, I have been to Paris, I have
been to London I go everywhere . . . I am, 'ow you say? – a
singer-actress . . . when I passed to the other world I was forty-
five. I've been over – who knows – over here there is no time . . .
I like to think of myself how I was but I came over . . . Oh, dear
God . . .*

DICK: *Doris, now go back as far as you can go.*

DORIS(panic stricken): *Pierre, get the horses, get the horses.
Come, come, I beg you. Go forward, go forward. Don't think,
just go forward. The voices tell me go forward!*

DICK: *Now, Doris, go back even further, before that life, before
France.*

(long pause – voice changes again, becoming deep and
husky)

DORIS: *My name is Zombombie. I am Zombombie. I was born in
Jamaica. In our village we were considered to be rich, we had two
cows. My father, Buwala, was chief, the beginning of the eighteen
dates they tell me to say . . . Then one day I was taken away.
Men with boats came, long boats not like our boats, big boats and
they tied us and took us on big boats. I never saw my family,
Buwala, my mother Minetwa, until I came to the spirit world
and then I was reunited with my family . . . I call my woman
Kata. Good woman, we had four . . . Don't cut me with the
whip . . . don't say anything . . . I have to, Kata, I can't let
them treat us this way . . . They've sold my oldest son. Master,
I've served you faithfully, do not sell my first-born. My master's
name is Bwana Brownlow, sugar, sugar, sugar, is all he thinks
about . . . But one day our time will come. Our time will
come . . .*

DICK: *Do you hear voices now?*

DORIS: *Yes, I hear voices. My father say, don't worry, one day our
time will come.*

DICK: *Can you go back now before France, before Joan, before
Pierre?*

DORIS: *I am going home, I am going home. Up to the top of the mountain; it is Tibet . . .*

(voice changes becoming slow, deep and cultured)

I am a lama. I am this child's guide. I am now going to take her to the place that I call home. It is the table of the world. She has often expressed the desire to see my homeland and while she is deep in this unconscious mind I am going to take her for one second so that she can see where I started my last existence.

(Doris' voice comes back)

I am coming Ramanov, I am coming . . .

(Deep voice again)

Come, my child, come, feel the peace and the tranquillity, you see you do not need to have a lot. We have milk from goats, we have grapes from the vines, we have everything, enough to exist on. Come, come into the quietness, come into the spiritual love that can surround you. This was my life and a little of this only can I give you in your lifetime. Sit upon the mountain, let your spirit soar high. Feel my sun light, open yourself, let your spirit free, let that almighty power and force flow into you.

(Doris' voice again)

Oh Ramanov, dear Ramanov. I am so sorry I disappoint you so often. I do try hard.

DICK: *Who is Ramanov?*

DORIS: *Ramanov is my guide and teacher but I have never seen him face to face till now. So beautiful, such love, such compassion; oh, Ramanov, hold me! Let me shrug off all the pressures of this world. Help me to keep my inner strength. Help me to find that spiritual level you expect of me . . .*

(Pause – then deep voice again)

And now I'm bringing her back, and to you my son, Shalom!

When I came round it was as if I'd just woken from a long refreshing sleep. Yet I still felt vague and pleasantly light-headed. Dick was smilng at me.

'How d'you feel, Doris?'

'Oh, I feel as if I've been asleep for a long time.'

'Can you remember anything about it?'

'No, I can't remember anything.' I stopped. At the edge of my mind a memory flashed away, like a fragment of a dream. I struggled to catch it. 'At least – oh, no – that can't be right. I felt very sad.' And Ramanov, I thought. Something to do with Ramanov. 'I've got a vague feeling I dreamt of Ramanov . . . that he took me somewhere . . . oh, it was incredible. It seemed as though it was the top of the world. The world looked very small, very insignificant. I think he was trying to tell me to put things into their proper perspective. Do you think that's possible?'

Dick thought it was. As he spoke, a sudden memory of his hands on my face came back.

'Dick, were you touching my face?' I asked. 'What were you doing?'

'I was wiping away the tears,' he said and showed me the pile of damp tissues he'd amassed during the regression.

He played the tape of the session, with my permission, of course, over the air. It was disturbing to hear it. I sounded so distressed and panic stricken at times, as if I really was reliving those terrible incidents. The funny thing is my voice changed quite distinctly every time a different person spoke and both Dick and John said that my face changed, too.

I have to admit I don't know what to make of it. Was I dreaming out loud or was I really recalling past lives? I don't suppose I'll find out till I get to the other side myself!

Another strange thing happened when I was staying with my friend Eileen, a singer who lives in a beautiful country house in Stourbridge. I'd gone down to Stourbridge to talk to the local spiritualists but since I hadn't long recovered from my operation for breast cancer and I was still rather low, Eileen asked me to spend a few days resting with her in the clean country air.

I was glad of the excuse. It was always lovely to see Eileen and as she'd only lost her husband, John, eighteen months before I thought I might be able to cheer her up a little.

I had a marvellous time. Eileen spoiled me shamelessly. She put me in John's old bedroom overlooking a green paddock and swaying sycamore trees. It was a striking room with black and white geometric wallpaper, which John, who had been an architect, had chosen himself.

I was not quite as fit as I thought I was. The meeting the first night exhausted me and when I got back Eileen took one look at my tired face and sent me straight to bed.

'Go on, Doris, you get to bed and I'll bring up a pot of tea. We can chat in the bedroom.'

I was thankful to do as I was told and, as good as her word, Eileen came up about ten minutes later with the tea. I was already pretty drowsy and the way I recall it we chatted for a while and then I thought I fell asleep. At any rate I don't remember a thing until I 'came to' about twenty minutes later. I'll let Eileen explain what happened next:

EILEEN: '*It was the strangest thing I've ever experienced and I'm certainly not given to imagining things. Doris wasn't really very well and I was determined she would have a good rest while she stayed with me. I got her to bed early that first night and we were talking over our tea, when suddenly Doris went silent. I thought she must have fallen asleep because she was terribly tired but when I looked at her I saw that her face had changed. It was the most extraordinary thing I've ever seen. It was as if a film had come down over her face, completely hiding her features, and over the top a man's face appeared.*

'*The skin was yellowish, the features sharp and clean cut and he was wearing a skull cap. I read a lot, particularly about foreign countries, and I'll swear I was looking at a Tibetan monk.*

'*I was amazed, absolutely fascinated. I really sat up in my chair wondering what would happen next. Then as I watched, the monk sort of dissolved, the features shifted and suddenly it was my late husband.*

'*Without a doubt it was John's face. He still looked drawn and ill, the way he did before he died and his hands were plucking at the bedclothes the way they used to. I just couldn't believe my eyes.*

' "John, that's not you, is it?" I asked.

'He was in one of his old, slightly querulous moods and snapped, "Who d'you think it is" and before I knew it, we were scrapping again!

' "Don't be cross, John," I said. "I wasn't expecting this."

'We talked for a while about my son, David, and John remarked on the fact that though I'd otherwise kept the bedroom exactly as he'd left it, I'd changed a lamp fitting. I suppose we must have been talking for nearly twenty minutes and then he seemed to go all tired and it was Doris again. The funny thing was she opened her eyes, saw the tea and said "Hello, dear – oh, lovely, you've brought my morning tea." She thought she'd been asleep all night and it was the next morning.

'There's an odd sequel to the story, too. The next morning when I did take Doris' tea in to her, she told me that John had come back to talk to her during the night. John knew a lot about art, his hobby was painting and apparently he spent half the night lecturing Doris on the use of colour.

' "Then he took me to see the painting he's working on at the moment," Doris said. "There was a big painting on an easel and, well, I've never seen anything like it. Great swirling patterns of the most brilliant colours that seemed to pulsate and absorb you right into the picture. I was drawn right in and out the other side. And when I went through the colours I felt much better."

'I thought it sounded like a marvellous dream, but later on I was talking to an old family friend whose name was also John and who happened to be staying in the room downstairs that night.

' "D'you know, I had a really vivid dream last night. I could have sworn I saw Doris walking through the room in the most beautiful dress of brilliant flowing colours."

'I can't explain any of these things. I don't know why they happened, or how they happened but, as I said before, I'm not the sort of person to imagine things. It definitely happened and I've seen nothing like it before or since.'

As you can see, the most exciting things seem to happen to me when I'm unconscious and completely unaware of what's going on. It's most frustrating! The lesser incidents are almost as interesting, however.

On one occasion I was visiting a journalist friend, Kay Hunter, at her beautiful seventeenth-century cottage in Suffolk. It was a lovely place, deep in the country, with oak beams and inglenooks. During the visit I popped upstairs to the bathroom.

Like the rest of the house, it had a low ceiling and oak beams but the sink, bath and towels were completely modern. I stood there washing my hands and staring at my hair in the mirror. It was looking really haywire again – I must get to the hairdressers soon, I was thinking, when my eyes seemed to go peculiar and my reflection slid out of the glass.

Shaking my head to clear it, I turned round in time to see the bathroom fade and another room take its place. I was standing in a bedroom. In front of me was a low truckle-bed covered with a patchwork quilt, and sitting on the bed was an old man.

'My name is George Baker,' he told me. 'You'll find that name in the deeds of the house.'

And then before my eyes, George and his bedroom turned paler and paler until they became transparent and I was back in the bathroom again.

My reaction was annoyance more than anything else.

'Honestly!' I said to my restored reflection in the mirror as I combed my hair, 'I can't even go to the bathroom without them bothering me!'

But all the same I mentioned it to Kay, who said she had long suspected that the bathroom had been converted from a former bedroom.

'It's far too big for a bathroom,' she said, and sure enough when she checked the deeds she found a George Baker.

Another time I was visiting Phil Edwards, our healer friend, who also lived in a beautiful old house. We were sitting in Phil's study, the bottom part of a split-level room, separated from the top by several steps.

Suddenly I looked up to see a baker coming down these steps. He had rosy cheeks as if he'd just come from his oven, there was flour on his face and he was dressed in white with a tall hat, not a small peaked hat like they wear nowadays.

Shall I say something or not? I wondered. I didn't want Phil to think I was one of those mediums who thinks she sees things wherever she goes but the baker just stood there on the steps, beaming round at all of us making it so obvious he wanted to be friends that I couldn't ignore him.

'Phil, you might think me a bit mad,' I ventured, 'but there's a baker standing on the steps.'

To my amazement Phil just laughed, moved back his armchair and said, 'I'm not at all surprised, Doris. You see this part of the house used to be the bakery,' and behind the armchair, he pointed out the original baker's oven which he'd kept in place.

Perhaps I've made it sound as if those sort of things only happen to me. Well of course they don't — I've also witnessed some odd things happening to other people.

Years ago, soon after we had lost our baby and before I realized I was a medium, John and I were investigating spiritualism, desperate to make contact with our son. Someone told us about a trumpet seance that was taking place not far from our home. John and I had no idea what a trumpet seance was but ever hopeful of some word about John Michael, we went along.

We were shown into a large room, bare but for a circle of chairs arranged around a trumpet on the floor. It was quite an ordinary trumpet that had been painted with luminous paint so that it would show up in the dark. Mediums who did this sort of work needed darkness, we were told.

This sounded like an excuse for trickery to John and I so we inspected the trumpet very carefully but there was no sign of ropes or cords. Then the medium, an ordinary looking middle-aged man, came in and asked if two of the ladies present would volunteer to stitch his jacket. Stitch his jacket? I thought. What's wrong with it? It doesn't look torn to me. So I volunteered out of sheer curiosity.

I was given the strange task of sewing the sleeves of his jacket to the sleeves of his shirt, while the other lady who had stepped forward was asked to stitch his jacket together all down the front. I did my work most thoroughly and when the medium was firmly sewn up he sat in a chair and two of the men tied his legs to the legs of the chair and his arms to the sides of it. This was certainly the most peculiar seance I'd ever been to!

Finally, when the man was trussed up like a Christmas turkey, we all sat down, a quiet prayer was offered, the door locked and the lights turned out. John and I waited in trepidation, wondering what on earth would happen next.

There was silence in the room and all eyes were drawn to the only point of light, the trumpet which glowed ghostly green-white on the floor. As we stared, the trumpet started to rise from the floor, faltered, fell back and then rose again, higher and higher until it was level with our faces.

Slowly it turned in the air until it was pointing at one of the men in the group and from nowhere a voice spoke to him of his family. Round the group it went heralding a message for each one of us, but when it came to me the words were confused. It sounded as if several people were trying to talk at once and I couldn't make out anything clearly. John got a proper message but it wasn't about John Michael. I realize now that we went there in the wrong frame of mind. All we were thinking was we must have our son, we must have our son, and therefore we blocked anyone else who was trying to get through to us. Not understanding this at the time, we were bitterly disappointed.

The seance lasted an hour and a half and when it was

over the trumpet fell to the floor again, the lights were put on and there was the medium tied to the chair, but in his shirt sleeves. His jacket lay nearby on the floor next to the trumpet – the stitches still intact. If that was a trick, I remain baffled to this day as to how it was done.

I know much more about this kind of work now. We call it physical mediumship because the medium produces physical phenomena: moving objects, or ectoplasm. You don't see many physical mediums these days, probably because it takes years to develop the gift and in this modern world we don't have the time to spare. I've since learned that physical mediums need to work in the dark or by an infra-red light because the energy they produce reacts badly to light and also for some reason to metal or electrical objects. If you were to switch on the light while the medium is working, or to produce something electrical, I've been told, you could badly injure him.

I've seen evidence of this myself. John and I were spending a weekend at Stansted Hall, the beautiful Jacobean style mansion in Essex where psychic courses are held throughout the year. Our visit coincided with the appearance of Gordon Higginson, an old friend who is also one of the greatest physical mediums alive today.

Gordon was giving some lectures and a seance at which he hoped to produce ectoplasm which would form itself into the features of the loved one who was communicating. These seances were always very popular and it was difficult to get a place, so John and I, who were both getting over severe bouts of 'flu, decided to let our seats go to other people.

'We're still feeling a bit wobbly,' I explained to Gordon, 'and if we're taken ill half-way through the seance we won't be able to get out.' The doors are always locked during seances to prevent people wandering in by mistake and switching on the light.

'All right, love,' said Gordon. 'I hope you feel better soon. I'll probably see you in the morning.'

Everyone else was going to the seance, so John and I went early to our room. The lovely old building fell absolutely silent as the seance got under way and I stretched out on the bed, enjoying the peace.

There in the countryside you couldn't hear a sound – not like our flat in a busy London street where cars and lorries roar past day and night.

John unpacked his healing book and settled quietly with that. The minutes ticked by and my eyes started to close. I shall really have to get up and undress if I'm going to sleep, I told myself lazily and was debating whether I could be bothered to move when there was a knock at the door.

'Who can that be?' I asked drowsily. 'I thought everyone was at the seance.'

I got up, smoothing my hair and opened the door. There was no one there. I'd taken a moment or two to answer so I stepped out onto the minstrel gallery and looked over the banisters so that I could see the staircase and the whole front hall. The place was deserted. There was not a soul in sight. Puzzled I went back in. 'That's strange. There's no one there,' I said to John. I sat down on the bed again, about to stretch out once more, when suddenly I froze.

'Something's happened to Gordon,' I cried, hardly knowing what I'd said till the words were out. I rushed to the door and ran out again just in time to hear a commotion downstairs. As I looked over the banisters I saw several men carrying Gordon out of the seance room.

We never did find out exactly what had happened, but apparently Gordon had forgotten he was wearing a metal buckle on his belt. There had been some disturbance during the seance which had caused the ectoplasm to return to Gordon's body with such force, his metal buckle had become red hot and burned him.

I went to see him when his friends had put him to bed. He looked dreadful. His face was crimson and he was too weak even to lift a cup of tea to his lips. Someone had put a plaster over the burn but knowing I was a trained nurse, Gordon asked me to have a look at the wound. Gently I peeled back the plaster. The burn looked very painful. The skin round the navel was angry red and bubbling with blisters.

'It's blistered, Gordon,' I told him. 'It's going to be pretty sore for a while. Come on, drink your tea and try to get some sleep. That's the best thing for you.'

As I left him to his painful night I thought to myself I wasn't a bit surprised that we have so few physical mediums left today. It's just not worth the risk.

Talking of Gordon reminds me of the time he decided to test me. He'd always been very close to his mother, Fanny Higginson, herself a wonderful medium, who taught him everything she knew.

After she passed, Gordon said to me, 'Doris, I'd like you to do a sitting for me, because if my mother's going to come back to anybody it would be to you.'

By coincidence, during the weekend of the funeral I was speaking at the church in Gordon's village and so he invited John and I to dinner.

It was a magnificent house standing in extensive grounds with a front and back drive. We went in through the large square hall full of plants and flowers and then Gordon took us into his own room, as he calls it, which looked to be like a very large lounge with picture windows and a bar. Gordon himself cooked a marvellous dinner and insisted on serving us with sherry and wine with liqueurs afterwards. I'm not used to drinking and I had to warn him that I wouldn't be able to work if I was tipsy.

'Nonsense,' Gordon protested. 'What's good enough for my mother is good enough for you, Doris. Oh, by the way, before you do my sitting I wonder if you could possibly do a couple of sittings for some friends of mine?'

'Well, I'll try,' I promised.

The curtains weren't drawn and as we sat there chatting I saw my first sitter arrive, a young girl who walked up the front drive from the main street. She rang the bell and Gordon went to let her in.

The girl seemed a little uneasy, and I assumed she had never had a sitting before but it went very well. Towards the end I asked 'Who's Gillian?'

'I'm Gillian,' she answered.

Then a few more details came through and I became confused. 'I think I'm talking to Gordon's mother,' I told the girl. 'She's talking about Gordon a lot, perhaps because we're in his house. She's also mentioning Gordon's shop – do you know the shop?'

'Oh, yes,' she said, 'I work in it.'

Then right at the end, Fanny said, 'That's *our* Gillian,' and I suddenly remembered that Gordon had a niece called Gillian who lived in the house with her husband and family. Gillian owned up at once.

'I didn't want to do it, Doris. I felt a bit guilty but Gordon persuaded me. I put on my hat and coat and went out the back door down the drive, along the road and up the front drive so that you wouldn't guess. Gordon wanted to make sure you see!'

I had to laugh. Trust Gordon to be so careful, but at least he was getting real evidence. We went back into the lounge and I scolded Gordon mildly over coffee. Then my next sitter arrived.

She was an older woman and she, too, looked a little apprehensive. I tuned in and we got under way, but after a while I realized I wasn't doing very well. Some of the names that were coming through sounded as if they belonged to the last sitter.

'I'm so sorry,' I said to the woman, 'I think I must be tired. It's quite late and I've just done a sitting. Maybe I'm getting mixed up.' But then without doubt I heard Fanny again.

'That's my daughter, Hazel,' she said firmly. 'And I want you to give my love to our Leslie.'

'That's my daughter,' Hazel admitted.

'Tell her I'm so glad I saw the baby before I came over, Doris,' Fanny went on, 'though I watch over her now.' She also mentioned the name Heather.

'Who's Heather?'

'Heather's my granddaughter,' said Hazel.

Gordon had done it again. Unknown to me he'd brought his sister along for the second sitting. He hadn't wanted a sitting himself at all because he felt that as I knew him so well the information I gave him couldn't be counted as evidence. Now, thanks to his elaborate precautions, he was quite sure that Fanny had come back.

CHAPTER 9

1980 turned out to be the busiest year of my life particularly the time I spent on my tour of Australia, New Zealand and Tasmania. It was incredibly hard work and it nearly killed me at one point, but I realized that it was all worthwhile. It was meant to be.

Looking back on the tour I find many blanks in my memory. Days blurred into one another, cities became indistinguishable, particularly as I went backwards and forwards on an erratic course, visiting some places more than once. But although the details have faded I am left with a few vivid memories and an overwhelming impression of warmth and love from tens of thousands of people. There were many times when I was so exhausted I didn't know how I could carry on but there were even more times when I was moved to tears by the affection and thoughtfulness of a complete stranger.

I hadn't visited Australia since 1978 and I couldn't help wondering if they would remember me, but the moment we walked into Melbourne airport, I knew it was going to be fine. Limp and bedraggled and seven hours late because of delays on the ground in Europe and Bombay, we were shuffling through immigration when a man looked into my face and said, 'Hello, Doris Stokes. How are you, mate?' and I felt as if I'd come home.

Outside, Tony, a driver from the Myers bookshop chain which was organizing our tour, was waiting with a sparkling limousine to take us to our hotel. 'Doris, will you give me nine numbers for the lotto?' he asked as we drove along.

I assumed this must be some kind of lottery, perhaps the Australian equivalent of our football pools or premium bonds.

'I don't really do that sort of thing, Tony,' I explained. 'If I could, I'd be a millionaire by now on the football pools.'

'Never mind. Just give me nine numbers,' Tony persisted. 'I've got a feeling.'

Laughing, I reeled off nine numbers completely at random. 'You'd do better with a pin,' I warned but strangely enough the next time we heard from Tony, he told us his numbers had come up. He hadn't won a great deal of money, only about thirty dollars, but he was absolutely thrilled.

The next day our routine began. There were television and radio interviews, phone-ins, live appearances and, most important of all, book signings at Myers book shops all over the country. We drove from store to store within cities sometimes doing three a day and we flew from city to city to repeat the performance. I must admit I had no idea what I was letting myself in for. I had imagined I would visit a bookshop, a little place like my local Smiths, autograph a few books and then wander off again. It wasn't like that at all.

The first morning we pulled up in front of an enormous, gleaming department store as wide as Harrods and seven storeys high. There were crowds of window shoppers outside and as we walked towards the entrance, they all ran across shouting: 'Hello, Doris. How are you?' and pushed in through the glass doors with us. I think this alarmed the organizers because after that we always went through the loading bay at the back.

I was led through the beautiful store, all airy open spaces and masses of green plants, to the restaurant. I thought perhaps we were going to have a quiet cup of tea before we started to work but instead I was confronted by two hundred people eating scones with jam and cream.

'They've come to have morning tea with Doris Stokes,' someone explained.

I stared at a mass of jammy faces all staring back at me. 'What am I suppose to do with them?' I whispered.

'Just talk to them for a few minutes and walk up and down a bit,' they said.

So I talked and I went from table to table saying hello to as many people as I could. This process was repeated in almost every store I visited and one of the nicest parts about it was the way mothers brought their children along to see me and everywhere I went I was given babies to hold and toddlers to cuddle.

That first morning I came upon a long table with about twenty people seated round it – three generations of one family!

They jumped up as I approached and made a great fuss of me. 'We wrote to you in 1978 and you sent us this,' they explained and proudly showed me a much handled sheet of paper. A lump came into my throat when I saw that it was only one of the standard letters we'd had printed because I couldn't possibly answer personally all the thousands of letters I'd received. On the back was one of my favourite verses: 'God enters the heart broken with sorrow and opens the door to a brighter tomorrow.' Then, before I'd recovered from the letter, they produced a flower. When I'd last toured Australia I was given so many flowers that I handed them out at my live shows to people who had received spirit messages.

'You gave us this in '78, Doris,' they said, 'and look at it.'

I stared down at a faded long stemmed carnation and though it was two years old it hadn't dried up or crumpled. It was still soft and supple and pretty and tears came into my eyes to think that they had treasured this little flower all that time simply because it came from me.

After the restaurant would come the book signing and usually I was led to the book department which had been specially cleared for the purpose and furnished with a little dais complete with table and chair. During my first session a dear little boy of two and a half clambered up onto the dais clutching a bunch of yellow flowers. 'For you, Auntie Doris,' he said, pushing them at me.

'Oh thank you, love,' I said hugging him. 'They're lovely,' and I searched in my pocket for a sweet but was disappointed to find I had none with me. After that I always asked for a bowl of sweets to be left on the table, and of course the children got to know about it. Most of the time I'd be sitting there signing away with children climbing all over my feet.

People would queue for hours to get their book signed. I noticed one boy of about seventeen, patiently shuffling forwards as the queue moved along and when he got to me he said, 'You know, Doris, I stood for four hours waiting to see my favourite pop group but this is more exciting.'

Bless your heart, I thought. 'What, more exciting to come and see an old granny than a pop group!' I teased.

'Yes,' he said solemnly, 'it is, and I've been here since nine this morning.'

Touched, I signed his book, but still he hovered. 'May I kiss you?' he asked shyly.

'Of course you can, love,' I said. So, blushing bright red, he bent, kissed me on the cheek and rushed away.

The next day I returned to the same store and there he was again with his autograph book!

Another time, in a shop in Sydney, the promotions girl on the dais with me touched my arm and said, 'There's a Father Jefferies who'd like a word with you.'

I turned and found a priest standing there. 'I would be very honoured if you would sign my book, Doris. I think it's beautiful,' he said. When I'd signed it he asked if he could give me a blessing.

'I'd like that very much, Father,' I said. So there, in the middle of the store, he gave me a blessing!

At another store on the outskirts of Sydney we were met by a very harassed manager. 'They've been queueing since eight-thirty,' he said. 'We can't take them in the book department or the restaurant so we've had to clear out the furniture department and put them in there.'

We walked in and I stopped dead in amazement. There were hundreds of people as far as I could see and it was obvious they had been waiting for a long time. They were sitting on the floor and mothers were changing their babies' nappies on the carpet. This was another nice thing: they didn't feel I was someone grand for whom they should put on a front. If their baby needed changing, they changed him, and if their baby wanted feeding, they fed him, knowing that it was only Doris and they didn't have to do anything different.

But the length of time people had to queue worried me. I would see young mothers standing for ages with a baby in their arms and another in a pushchair; and old people, crouched on sticks. So I always used to ask the crowd if they would let mothers with babies, old people and any sick people who couldn't stand very well come up first. There was never any fuss. The crowd would always part to let them through with good humour.

Still the little gifts came. One lady came up and put a parcel on the table for me. I'd mentioned in my last book the very special meaning that sky-blue velvet has for me and she'd obviously remembered this.

'Doris, I tried very hard to get some blue velvet for you,' she said, 'but I couldn't so I got the next best thing.'

When I opened the parcel I found a tin of blue velvet talcum powder and of course that set me off crying all over again.

Other people baked us cakes or gave us chocolates and flowers but with all the hotel meals and the constant travelling we couldn't eat them or keep them. I used to give them away and one time one of our drivers, a lovely boy called Paul, said, 'You know it's a good thing my wife's seen you on TV and she knows who I'm with or she'd wonder what I was up to coming home with chocolates and flowers every night!'

Of course I was often aware as I sat there signing till my arm ached and the pages swam before my eyes, that the person standing next to me was desperately hoping for a contact. It would have been impossible to work for everyone, but just occasionally their loved one came through so vividly that I had to repeat what I was hearing.

At other times people had travelled so far in hope, I couldn't refuse to tune in to find some little scrap that might help. One lady told me she'd travelled three hundred and ninety miles. I couldn't turn her away. It was the same at public meetings. At one a man stood up and said he and his wife had come five hundred miles for a message. Hadn't I got anything for them?

It was question time but I couldn't refuse a plea like that. I tuned in. 'You've lost a child, haven't you?' I asked.

'Yes, we have,' he agreed.

'That's odd,' I said. I could hear a little girl's voice but she was giving me a boy's name. It was quite definite, however, so I went on. 'Well, I'm sure it's a girl I can hear but she says her name is Bobby.'

'That's right,' said the man. 'That's all we wanted,' and he sat down again.

Question time continued but ten minutes later Bobby returned.

'My *real* name is Roberta,' she explained. We were in mid question at that point but I said, 'Excuse me,' and turned again to the direction where the man and his wife were sitting.

'By the way, Bobby has just told me that her real name is Roberta,' I said. They both burst into tears.

'Doris,' said the man, 'it was worth every mile of the way to know you can tell us we've lost a daughter and her correct name.'

It was all he wanted. Such a tiny piece of information meant so much. It was touching the way so many people were satisfied with so little. On another occasion during question time, two young girls stood up, one supporting the other who was weeping.

'Doris, can you do anything for my friend?' begged the more composed of the two. 'She lost her baby two weeks ago and she's been like this ever since. She's too upset to speak to you.'

I thought of John Michael and my heart went out to the ashen-faced girl sobbing into her handkerchief. There were no words to express the pain and grief she must be going through but I knew, I knew.

In my head a woman's voice said, 'The baby's name is Robin.'

'Is the baby called Robin?' I asked.

'Oh yes, yes!' cried the girl, looking up in wonder.

'Well, don't worry, darling. He's quite safe. His grandmother says he's with her and she's looking after him for you. He's well and happy.'

And the young mother sat down again, content just to know that her baby was in good hands.

Then there were all the shows – far too many to recall in detail but I started with a radio phone-in presented by my old friend, the cheeky Bert Newton. To my surprise, while we waited to go on the air, a waiter arrived with a china tea service, a silver pot and a plate of sandwiches on a tray. I had to laugh because the first time I went on his show in 1978 I was given coffee in a paper cup.

'What's this in aid of, Bert?' I joked, holding up the silver pot. 'Does it mean I've come up in the world?'

' 'Course it does,' he said, helping himself to a sandwich. 'Only the best for Doris Stokes. We wouldn't dare do anything else!'

During the programme I was in the middle of a message when another voice cut in. 'There's been a fire,' it said. 'There's five of us. It's only just happened.'

The woman I was talking to couldn't place it at all. 'No, I'm sorry, Doris,' she apologized. 'I don't know anyone who's been in a fire.'

'Don't apologize, love,' I said. 'I've got a crossed wire somewhere. It's not your fault.' But the voice kept coming back during the commercial break and it was most insistent about the fire. I discussed it with Bert.

'I can't understand it, Bert. It seems so positive and they say it's only just happened.'

'It wasn't something you saw in the paper or anything, was it?' Bert asked.

I shook my head. 'We only arrived in the early hours this morning and we came straight to the studio when we got up. I haven't seen a paper since we left London.'

The producer sent out for a paper just in case, and in the next break he passed it to me. There it was. Fire had broken out in a caravan and five people had gone over together.

The next show I did was the Don Lane Show. When we walked onto the set Don was already rehearsing for the night show but as soon as he saw me, he leapt up, as handsome and slim as ever, gave me a big hug and swung me round until I was breathless.

It was so nice to see him again I felt all weepy. You'll have to pull yourself together, Doris, I told myself sternly. The way things were going I'd spend the whole tour in tears if I carried on like this.

Don had got a new set since I had last been on the show. In place of the smart green and tan set he used to have was a beautiful affair of soft violets and greys, but I eyed the graceful steps that wound down the centre of it in dismay. I couldn't help remembering the last time I'd been on his show when I concluded my appearance with a spectacular fall down the steps behind the set, and was obliged to go back to say goodbye with a bruised ankle and laddered tights!

'Don, I haven't got to come down those steps on camera have I?' I asked gloomily, imagining a repeat performance.

'Not if you don't want to, love,' said Don.

'I'd rather not,' I said. 'It takes me all my time not to tread on my dress. I'm sure I'd go flying.'

'That's all right,' Don assured me. 'We'll fix up a curtain or something and you can come straight onto the floor from behind that.'

Relieved, I went off to get ready and when it was my time to appear I was amazed to find they had not only rigged up a special curtain but they had also built a step at the side of the set covered with the same grey carpet for me to stand on while I waited to appear.

Unfortunately my first two contacts weren't promising. I began with a Scottish lady who said her name was McCarthy. Nobody in the audience could place her. She was crystal clear, however, and gave me several more family names but it was no use, nobody claimed her and I had to move on.

Next I got a little boy. He was called Peter and he said he'd passed with leukaemia. I described him carefully but again no one claimed him. 'What a shame,' I said. 'He's only a few years old and he thinks somebody here belongs to him.' But there was no response. Sadly I had to tell Peter we'd had no luck and pass to someone else.

I was getting a bit worried by this time that the demonstration would be a disaster but fortunately, after Peter, the messages were claimed in the normal way.

After I came off after the show, the floor manager called me over. 'Look Doris,' he said and pointed to a man in the orchestra who was blowing his nose hard on a large white handkerchief. 'It was his nephew, Peter, who died of leukaemia. He didn't like to say anything.'

'Well, thank goodness for that,' I said. 'The little boy was so insistent that he knew somebody in the studio, I wondered what was wrong.'

And the mystery of my Scottish McCarthy was solved a few days later. Don received a letter from a woman who had recently lost her husband. Desperate to believe, she'd pulled up her chair in front of the television set and sent out her love to all her relatives and friends in the spirit world, just as I advised, and straight away my message came. Her name was McCarthy and I'd given her mother's name and the names of her brothers. It had worked even though she wasn't in the studio.

Another memorable show was the John Singleton Show in Sydney. I'd heard a lot about John Singleton. He was a real 'Oker' I was told beforehand which apparently means a real Australian. He was very rich, arriving at the studios in his own helicopter and since it was his show he believed in saying exactly what he thought. John Singleton doesn't mince his words, I was warned. You either love him or hate him.

We drove along through steep hills and valleys and by the time I reached the studios perched on top of a hill with a breathtaking vista of green, I was very intrigued to meet this Mr Singleton.

It wasn't long before I got my wish. We'd hardly got inside the building when we couldn't fail to notice a tall, broad man with corn coloured hair and full evening dress including a dickie bow tie, striding down the corridor.

'Hello, Doris,' he said, taking my hand in his great rock-like grasp and shaking it up and down. 'Come into my dressing room.'

There was much twittering and fluttering in the background over this and I understood that a great honour had been conferred.

We were led into a plush room with enormous black leather armchairs and a settee, and there John Singleton chatted with great courtesy. There was no trace of the difficult, possibly abrasive man I'd been led to expect and throughout our meeting he was charming.

I wasn't allowed to demonstrate on John's show, I was told, because I was already booked to do so on a rival show and for some reason they wouldn't let me do both. This seemed rather unfair to me but John didn't seem to mind. He was content to talk about my book and ask me questions. Then he said:

'Doris, you remember that poem in your book about your baby?'

'Yes,' I replied. How could I forget it? While I was still grieving badly for my little John Michael, I'd heard a voice reciting a poem. That poem had given me so much comfort it was never far from my mind during the thirty years since.

'Do you think you could recite it for us now?'

'Yes, of course,' I said and went straight into those well loved lines:

In a baby castle just beyond my eye,
My baby plays with angel toys that money cannot
    buy.
Who am I to wish him back,
Into this world of strife?
No, play on my baby,
You have eternal life.

At night when all is silent
And sleep forsakes my eyes
I'll hear his tiny footsteps come running to my side.
His little hands caress me, so tenderly and sweet
I'll breathe a prayer and close my eyes and embrace
    him in my sleep.

Now I have a treasure that I rate above all other,
I have known true glory – I am still his mother.

When I'd finished, John invited questions from the audience. 'Excuse me, Doris,' he said, 'you carry on talking,' and he went over to the band and spoke to them for a few seconds. Then he came back.

'I've asked the band to play very softly a piece of music called *No Greater Love*,' he said and even as he spoke the band started to play. 'I wonder, Doris, if you could recite your poem to the music.'

So I recited my poem once more as the music swayed in the background and there was not a sound in the studio. The words and the music combined to create an atmosphere so beautiful that it was difficult to speak and my voice faltered several times, but I struggled on. Finally the last line fell away into dazed silence. For several seconds no one spoke or moved and the programme ended quietly. I was too full of emotion to say much more.

The next day a box almost as long as my coffee table at home arrived at the hotel. I lifted the lid with trembling fingers to find a mass of velvety orchids inside – with love from John Singleton.

There is a lovely sequel to this story. Months later, long after I'd arrived home, the postman delivered a hard, flat parcel to my door. It was covered in brown paper but it must have had 'picture' written on the outside because I heard Terry moan from the kitchen, 'More stuff to dust!'

It was covered with bright New Zealand stamps, however, so I took no notice of him and tore into it excitedly. On a dull, winter's day it was like a little piece of New Zealand sunshine. Inside was one of the most beautiful gifts I've ever received: in flowing black copperplate writing on a gold background with the merest suggestion of flowers and babies on it, and framed in an ornate gold frame with scroll-work at the corners, was a copy of my poem.

The artist explained in an accompanying letter that he'd been so moved by my recital on the John Singleton Show that he'd felt inspired to set the poem down permanently for me. He only hoped he had got all the words correct. He had, and to this day that lovely picture hangs on the wall above the mantelpiece in my flat – a really treasured possession.

Another show that stands out in my mind is Hayden Sarjeant's Show in Brisbane. The Sarjeant Report. Hayden was a former minister, I was told, and likes to cover serious topics, but he allowed me to get on with my work in my usual way. In fact, he had invited so many people to the studio that the seats had to be arranged in stands like a football stadium and even then there were dozens of people sitting on the floor at the front.

The communications were coming through so well that I over-ran my allotted time but no one wanted me to stop. The producer kept saying, 'Carry on, we'll give you an extra five minutes,' and when that five minutes was up: 'Oh well, just five minutes more.' In the end he shrugged his shoulders: 'We might as well get it all in the can and use it later!'

During one of these periods of extra time, I was craning my head in an effort to find my next recipient. She was in the front somewhere, I was informed, but I couldn't see her.

'What's the matter, Doris?' asked Hayden, noticing my difficulty. 'Do you want to be up there with the audience?'

Even as he spoke I saw a light hovering over the head of a lady in glasses.

'No, it's all right. The lady I want is that lady there in glasses – I can see her from where I'm sitting.'

The cameras started to roll, but suddenly I heard Ramanov's voice. 'No it's not her. *Behind* her,' and I stood up abruptly.

'What are you doing? I thought you said it was all right sitting down,' said Hayden.

'Well, I thought it was,' I explained. 'Sorry, dear,' I hastily added to the disappointed lady in glasses, 'it's not you, they tell me, it's somebody sitting behind you, somebody I can't see from here.'

I climbed down and walked into the audience and, sure enough, behind this woman was another lady in sunglasses. As I looked at her I heard a young man saying that his name was Steven. The woman gasped. It was her son.

'I did it myself, you know,' Steven told me. Quickly I looked up at the cameras all round us. I couldn't say *that* out loud for everyone to hear. So I bent down and whispered, 'Did he take himself over?'

The woman's hands flew to her mouth and she nodded, biting her lip.

The message went on giving several family names and details and then right at the end Steven said proudly, 'I left sixty-three dollars.'

When I repeated this the woman gasped in amazement. 'Oh, my God!' she cried.

'Is that correct?' I asked.

'Yes. Yes, it is,' she said. 'We found it in a bottle in his wardrobe. Sixty-three dollars exactly.'

After the programme came to an end, people were milling about asking me to sign copies of the book. I was chatting and scribbling busily but at one point I happened to glance up and I saw Steven's mother deep in conversation with Hayden. A few minutes later Hayden came over.

'That's amazing, Doris,' he said. 'I know Steven's mother – the family are neighbours of mine. But I had no idea they were coming today. They didn't tell me.' The next morning he announced on his radio show that he personally could vouch for the accuracy of my message because he knew the family and everything I told them had been true.

By this time of course the pace of the tour was beginning to tell on me. I'm over sixty, after all, and not as fit as I used to be and, to be fair, I think even a younger person would have found it a strain. We dashed from place to place, from hotel to car to plane and back again, from store to studio to press conference with scarcely a break for meals. At one point lunch was a sandwich and a cup of coffee in the back of the car. The few days off I'd been allocated were rapidly eaten up by interviews, and I suppose I made it worse by being unable to refuse all those desperate eyes. When they looked at me with such hope, I couldn't just keep my head down, scribble *Doris Stokes* and get on my way.

I felt utterly exhausted. My voice was strained and croaking with all the talking I'd been doing, my right arm, weakened from my mastectomy operation used to swell up like a balloon from all the signing. I suppose I've never known when to stop and I pushed myself on and on trying to meet every demand that was made of me.

At last in Brisbane, after a two hour Press conference, I was led into a store for my second signing session of the day in the book department. There was a little dais covered in pale blue carpet on which stood a Queen Anne chair in matching blue velvet. It looked lovely but I noticed wearily that there were about six steps leading to the dais, which meant that once up there, I had to bend almost double to shake people's hands and take their books from them.

I'd already had a hectic day but I gritted my teeth and steeled myself to get on with it. Once up on the dais it was even worse than I had feared. The people crushed below me, at least ten deep and, as always, I found myself thinking, what do they want? What do they expect from me? I can't possibly help them all. Yet I hated to disappoint them. Every time I bent down the floor seemed to swing up and sideways and I could hardly reach the books that were offered.

Then for the first time in ages, I heard my father's voice. Loud and clear, it cut through all the surrounding chatter: 'Dol, get down from there.'

I was in the middle of speaking to someone so I tried to bring the conversation to a close but my father's voice came through again: 'Dol, get down from there *At Once*.' When Father was in that mood there was no disobeying him. Covered in confusion, my head spinning and the room around me a blur, I tried to stand up.

'I'll have to get down from here,' I muttered. 'I must get down.'

From somewhere in front of me a voice said, 'Goodness, what's the matter with Doris?'

'Doris, your face has gone crimson,' cried someone else.

Two men stepped forward, I felt myself half lifted down the steps, the chair was brought down from the dais and I collapsed thankfully into it. A glass of water was put into my hand.

'Are you all right?'

'Yes – I think so,' I mumbled, not really sure. 'I thought I was going to fall.'

A few minutes later, without knowing how it happened, I found myself signing books again. I've no idea what I wrote. I sat there moving my hand automatically across the pages. My head was going round like a clock and I couldn't quite remember where I was.

The next thing I knew I was back at the hotel feeling most peculiar. I wasn't quite so dizzy but there was this out-of-balance, not-quite-there sensation. I could see the room about me but somehow it seemed a long way off.

'Are you sure you're all right, love?' John kept asking but his voice came from a great distance as if he was speaking down a long tube.

I had a hot bath and went to bed. At least with my eyes closed and the curtains drawn, the room didn't seem so far away.

The next morning I felt a bit better, or at least I thought I did. The point was academic in any case because I had to get up to do a radio phone-in with Hayden Sarjeant. I got to the studio without incident and congratulated myself. I didn't feel too bad really. There was no pain anywhere, just this strange detached feeling as if I only had one foot in reality. There was also this strange inability to take in what people were saying. I gave up trying to follow conversations and concentrated on saying 'Yes' every now and again. No one seemed to notice.

The phone-in went ahead as planned and that was when I noticed another strange thing. As well as not being able to follow other people's conversations, I couldn't follow my own. I heard myself talking but for the life of me I couldn't understand what I was saying. It might have been complete gibberish for all I knew. I glanced at Hayden to see if he'd noticed anything amiss, but he was talking smoothly into the microphone, his face unruffled.

At last, during the commercial break, I said, 'Hayden, does it make sense to you what I'm doing?'

'What d'you mean, love?' asked Hayden.

'Well, half the time I don't know what I'm saying.'

'Well, you're right on the button,' he assured me. 'That last call was from a woman who had lost her daughter. You told her the girl's name was Caroline, she was nineteen and how she had died. Then the mother said there was one more thing she was waiting for and if you got that you'd save her sanity. You came back with "Caroline says to tell you she's got her teddy bear with her" and the mother burst into tears. Apparently she'd put the teddy bear in the girl's coffin.'

'Oh good. That's okay then,' I said vaguely. I didn't recall a word of it but if it was working it didn't matter. Hayden was staring at me rather strangely now, but the break was over. I fumbled for the headphones and pushed them back over my hair.

Hayden was still looking at me. I opened my mouth to say something to him but somehow I couldn't think of anything to say.

'All right. That's it!' he cried suddenly. 'Take those headphones off. That's it.'

Confused, I looked around. What was wrong?

'Jane!' Hayden yelled into the office behind the studio. 'Doris is ill. She needs a doctor. She's not leaving this building until she's seen one.'

The next few hours are a blur. I drank tea, I recall, and at some point a doctor examined me.

'It could have been one of three things,' he said. 'It could have been a stroke, a mild heart attack or . . .' and he mentioned some other complicated medical name that I can't remember. Eventually he came to the conclusion that

144

I was totally exhausted and an artery had closed in my head shutting off the oxygen flow.

'You need a good rest,' he said. 'You must have forty-eight hours doing nothing at all.'

That was a Friday. I spent the rest of the day in my room. Saturday we were put on a plane to Sydney – the next place on our itinerary. I rested for the weekend and by Monday I was ready to work again. Not as well as I might have been but I could cope.

One of the nicest things about Sydney was the fact that an old friend of mine, Alice Chaikovsky, lived there. I'd first met Alice when she was on holiday with her friend, Betty, in England.

Alice had spent three months visiting SAGB, Stansted Hall and other spiritualist places hoping to get a message but had had no luck at all. On her last night, she decided to go to one final demonstration at the SAGB and it happened to be the very night I was asked to take over at the last minute because the advertised medium was ill.

Alice told me afterwards that when it was announced the medium couldn't be there and Doris Stokes would take over instead, she thought, oh no, my last night wasted. But the second person I spoke to was Alice.

'I've got someone here who's speaking either Polish or Russian,' I explained. I don't speak any other languages but over the years I've got to recognize the sound of different languages. This man confused me, however. Part of the time it sounded like Polish and part of the time, Russian.

'That's all right!' cried Alice. 'He's Polish but he speaks Russian.'

'Who's Alice?' I asked.

'That's me!' cried Alice practically jumping up and down.

'Well, I've got Michael here,' I went on.

'That's my husband!'

Michael explained that Alice lived in Sydney, Australia.

He told me where he'd left his money and that he wanted a Russian church to be built with it, then he went on to describe an icon he wanted made. He talked about Stanislaus and Swchitz.

'I can't understand this,' I said. 'I thought he said he was a baker or something to do with bakeries but now he's saying it's something to do with the airport.'

'That's right,' said Alice, 'we make all the cakes and things for the airport.'

Finally Michael said, 'Will you tell Alice I've met Edie Turner.'

Alice was thrilled with it all. They don't usually get excited at SAGB but she was standing up and turning round to the audience saying, 'Isn't she marvellous? Isn't she good?'

Afterwards she was waiting on the steps outside and insisted on paying for my taxi home. We've been friends ever since.

Throughout our stay in Sydney, Alice kept inviting us to her house but our schedule was so tight we had to turn her down, very sadly, every time. Then just as we were about to leave for New Zealand, there was an air strike. We were delighted and packed our bags for Alice's instead.

Alice's house turned out to be very large with a verandah running round it with a big garden, which she called a yard, full of grapefruit, orange and lemon trees. The sight of citrus fruit hanging from the trees never ceased to amaze me and I loved to wander through the garden staring at it. To be allowed to pick a grapefruit was a wonderful treat.

It was marvellous to see Alice and Betty again. They were both confirmed spiritualists by now and Betty had developed a talent as a psychic artist. She's had no art training, she told me, and had never been good at art, but as she became involved in spiritualism she began feeling a tremendous urge to draw on a sheet of paper with coloured chalks. It grew so strong that she went out and bought the materials and, to her amazement, she produced a good picture.

Since then she's never looked back and she showed me some of her work. The detail was marvellous. One picture showed a woman wearing a lace shawl round her head and every whorl and loop of the pattern was as clear and sharp as if it had been real. In another picture of a mother and baby, every crease of the baby's arms and legs is shown in life-like detail.

Betty was particularly glad to see me because she'd been longing to tell me about her house in Spain. I had forgotten but apparently Betty had come to me in London for a sitting and I had told her that she was going to live in Spain in a house on a hill which looked as if it was pink-washed. At the time Betty thought this most unlikely but now she'd bought a Spanish house, standing on a hill. It was white, she explained, but when the sun is setting the walls are bathed in pink light and they look as if they've been pink-washed!

We were very sad to say goodbye to Alice and Betty when the strike ended, but as we drove once more to the airport I began to feel a twinge of excitement. I'd always wanted to visit New Zealand, and I had another wonderful friend there – my old student, almost my adopted daughter – dear Judy . . .

CHAPTER 10

To tell you about Judy I must first go back a few years to talk about my 'psychic evening classes' as they were nicknamed by one reporter.

When I was still working at SAGB in London, I was asked if I would take a teaching class. These classes usually consist of about twelve fledglings, as they're called – ordinary people from all walks of life who have become interested in spiritualism and want to develop their psychic gift.

This is quite possible to do because, as I've said before, everyone has got the spark within them and with practice it can be brought out. This doesn't necessarily mean that the student will become a brilliant medium. After all, you can probably teach most people to play the piano but only a very few would become concert pianists.

The teacher can't teach the student how to use his gift, only his guide knows what he is capable of, but her role is to help build up the atmosphere and give all her power to the fledglings, to tune in to what they are getting and help them sort it out. At first it's difficult to distinguish what's coming from your own mind and what's coming from the other side. The teacher can unscramble the message and help the fledglings reach their full potential.

I'd always believed in training the young. I often felt that if there had been more help around when I was young I could have saved so much time and mistakes instead of blundering around in the dark on my own. Who knows what I might have achieved if I'd started on my way earlier? So now that I had gained knowledge and experience I was only too pleased to do what I could to help the mediums of the future.

There was only one question I asked when a person

applied to join the class: why did they want to do it? And I only accepted one answer: because they wanted to serve, they wanted to help other people. I soon got to know whether they were telling the truth or not, but the great majority of youngsters who came to me were genuine, loving people who wanted to help others.

Poor health forced me to give up my regular job at SAGB. I told the class they could join other groups but they begged to stay with me and we ended up hiring a room in Fulham Town Hall, not far from my flat, for our weekly 'evening classes'.

The members of the class were my pride and joy. I was just as new to teaching as they were to learning so I drew on my own mistakes and Ramanov's advice in my efforts to create 'lessons'. I remembered the only teaching class I'd ever attended, years ago, when I'd been told to uncross my legs and hold my hands in a certain position. I'd spent the whole evening concentrating so hard on adopting the right posture I'd completely failed to make any contact at all.

It hadn't worked for me and I was determined not to clutter up my kids' minds with a lot of dos and don'ts. I kept the class as simple as possible. One of them would say a prayer offering ourselves to God in service, then we would join hands round the big oval table and I would tell them to forget the outside world and tune in to each other. 'Just think about the person on either side of you and send out all the love you can.' In this way the circle of love went round the table and this built up the psychic power. You could feel it getting stronger with every passing moment and when I felt it was strong enough I would drop my hands. Not a word was spoken but they would drop their hands around the table and we would get on with the work.

One young man was a yoga fan and he asked if it would be all right if he did his breathing exercises because he felt it helped him.

'Son, you can do whatever you like as long as it's not stupid or intended to draw attention to yourself,' I told him and so he used to sit there very quietly with his hands on his solar plexus doing deep breathing, and before long the rest of us found that we were doing it too! He was right: it did help and it proved to me that we can all learn something from each other. I'd always had trouble making myself relax and that young boy taught me how.

As the class tuned in, they used to tell me that my father was there and he began the lesson by drawing a big letter 'S' in the air above my head. I hadn't told them beforehand that my father's name was Sam as this proved to me that Dad was there, giving a helping hand with my teaching.

Often the students found their messages confusing and I explained what Ramanov had taught me. 'If you're given something you don't understand and the person you're talking to doesn't understand it either, test it,' I said. 'Suppose they are showing you a picture of a man on a black horse and this doesn't mean anything to you. Test the individual details. Say to yourself, it's not a black horse it's white, white. And back will come, it's a *black* horse. So you know the horse part of the picture is correct.'

One boy, Maurice, knew what he wanted to say but he had difficulty putting it into words. I don't know where the idea came from, but one night, watching him struggle, I said silently, 'Write it on the carpet for him,' and immediately Maurice leaned forward and started reading invisible words off the carpet.

The technique came in useful for other students, too. I used to invite mystery guests along for the evening from time to time because the students got to know each other so well it became even more difficult to judge whether their message came from the other side or their own subconscious. One evening my guest was a journalist called Frank Durham.

'Can you do anything for our friend here?' I asked the class.

There was a long silence. The big old clock on the wall ticked loudly and I could feel the intense concentration round me.

'I hear the name Frances William,' said Alice.

'Well, my name is Frank William,' said Frank.

They gave him a few more bits and pieces, then Frank asked them a question. 'I've been away recently,' he said. 'Could you ask the spirit world where I've been?'

There was another silence. The answer came to me, maddeningly loud and clear but I wasn't allowed to say anything. The silence continued and it was getting painful.

'Show them a picture,' I asked the spirit world silently. 'Put it on the table,' and suddenly Sandra, a schoolteacher, said, 'That's extraordinary!'

'What is?' I asked.

'Well, the table's filled with Flanders poppies,' she said.

Frank Durham nearly fell off his chair. 'That's where I've been,' he cried in astonishment. 'Flanders Fields, to do an article.'

When there were no guests, the class frequently demonstrated their growing powers by giving me evidence. The most striking concerned my old friend Harry Edwards. I mentioned Harry in my last book. He was one of the greatest healers we've ever had in Britain. It was Harry who helped me cure John of cancer – or should I say I helped him – and it was Harry who helped me recover with remarkable speed from my mastectomy operation without the need for radiation therapy.

I visited Harry shortly before he passed over, at his healing sanctuary in Surrey. It was a beautiful old manor house on a hill, with peaceful gardens leading down to open countryside. We strolled in the garden and took photographs, then Harry said, 'Come in here, Doris. I'd like to show you something.'

He led me through the house into a part I'd never seen before, then opened a gothic arched door to reveal a long low room with a vaulted ceiling very much like a church.

'This would make a wonderful church, Harry,' I said, gazing round. There was a great deal of richly carved wood, gleaming with care, and the walls were covered with paintings. Outside of an art gallery, I'd never seen so many paintings in one place. I peered closely at them. They were original oils and they were very good.

'These are beautiful, Harry,' I said, wondering how he could afford so many lovely things.

'I painted them myself,' he said nonchalantly.

'*Really?*' I examined them even more carefully. 'I didn't know you had a talent like this Harry. They're marvellous.'

Harry put his arm round my shoulders. 'I'll let you into a secret,' he whispered. 'They're all done by numbers!' and we both roared with laughter.

Months later, after Harry had passed, the class was gathered round the large oval table beneath the clock. An intense silence filled the room and I knew that several students had received communicatons but were struggling to sort out their impressions.

'I get the impression of a man standing behind you, Doris,' said Julie. 'He's got very white hair, a chubby round face and a sweet smile.'

Immediately Harry Edwards sprang to mind. It was a perfect description of him, but I thought I'd better wait for more conclusive proof.

'Can anyone else give me something more definite?' I asked.

'I can see a very large garden,' said one of the other girls slowly. 'It stands very high so I feel as if I'm looking out over the coutryside. Now I'm going under a rose arch and there's a fish pond with wire netting over it.'

I knew then, without doubt, that Harry Edwards was trying to get through to them. He had just shown them the grounds of his healing sanctuary.

'Yes,' I said. 'That's very good. I know who it is, but I'm waiting for more.'

'I hear the name Harry,' said Sandra suddenly. 'It's not Harry Edwards, is it, Doris?'

I said, 'Well, I think so, but we need something more to clinch it,' and in my mind I said, 'Give the kids more proof, Harry, so they can be absolutely certain.'

A few moments later one of the girls said, 'I get the impression I'm standing at the door of a church.'

'Well, there's a church in the village,' I pointed out, as indeed there are in most villages.

.'No,' the girl persisted. 'I don't think it's that sort of church. I get the impression of a long building and a lot of pictures.'

Instantly the memory of that afternoon when Harry had shown me his special room flashed into my mind.

'And he keeps saying tell Doris about the numbers,' said Sandra in a puzzled voice. 'I'm sure that's what he's saying. Tell Doris about the numbers.'

They'd got it! I knew then without doubt that Harry had made contact with the class.

I was very fond of all my students but the one I grew to love best was Judy. She was a pretty New Zealand girl, tall and slim with fair hair that had a touch of red in it. She wasn't going to develop into the best medium in my class, I knew that, but she was warm and lovable and when I first met her, very depressed.

Many things had gone wrong in her life and I suppose, with most of her relatives on the other side of the world, she was looking for someone to turn to. I was glad to help. We spent many an hour discussing her problems over a cup of tea after the class and gradually a real friendship blossomed.

Judy used to take me shopping and talk me into buying more up to date clothes. If I was ill, my health has always been erratic, she would do my shopping for me and being a great believer in herbal medicines she would also rush round with her health remedies and a list of instructions of what I should take and when. I'd always wanted a daughter and in a way Judy became the daughter I never had.

One morning she was at the flat, terribly upset about something or other and as she was explaining, her voice seemed to fade. I could see her lips moving but the sound was gone and over the top I could hear another voice.

'Judy,' I interrupted her, 'you're going back to New Zealand and you're going to marry a New Zealand man and have two babies.'

For a couple of seconds she was speechless with amazement. Then she laughed. 'Oh Doris, even if I wanted to I couldn't go back to New Zealand. I can't afford the fare!'

'Well, believe me, you will and you'll get married there,' I replied.

As I've told people many times, I'm not a fortune teller, but occasionally, when a sitter is very depressed and can't see any prospect of life improving, the relatives on the other side will sometimes give them a tiny glimpse of the good things in store to show them that things will get better. When this happens it is always correct and while I was very pleased that Judy was going to get married and have children, I was sorry that she was going away.

Judy took it lightly, however. The months passed and she remained as broke as ever and even if she'd won the football pools I don't think she would have rushed back to New Zealand. She was reasonably happy in Britain and didn't think that going back would improve her life in any way.

Then out of the blue one day she got an urgent phone call. There was trouble at home and she was needed badly. 'I can't afford the fare,' Judy told her relatives, but an aunt sent her the money.

The parting was very sudden. 'I'll be back just as soon as this is all cleared up,' Judy promised.

'You won't, you know,' I told her sadly.

'I will, I will,' she cried, throwing her arms round my

neck. 'There's nothing to keep me in New Zealand. I like it in England.'

I didn't want to distress her any more so I just smiled and said nothing. We parted with tears and promises to exchange letters very often.

At first Judy's letters were full of plans for what she would do when she returned to London. Then they became less frequent and finally she wrote to tell me she was marrying a man named McCarthy. Some time later there was a letter with the wonderful news that she now had a little girl called Trinity and later still came news of a son, called Sam, after my father.

That touched me very deeply and when I heard we were going to New Zealand in 1980 I was thrilled because it meant we'd have the chance of meeting Judy and her little family.

The first time I saw Australia I fell in love with it because it was so beautiful. Well, when I went to New Zealand where we were looked after by Sharon and Rolf Smith as if we were part of the family, I fell in love all over again. It was the middle of winter but everything was still so green and fresh. There were palm trees and even a few flowers in bloom and the air was sparkling clean. You could feel it doing you good every time you breathed. Whenever we got out of doors which unfortunately wasn't as often as we would have liked, John and I took great lungfuls of air to 'set us up' for our return to the carbon monoxide of London.

I'd been a bit worried during the tour because just before we left we'd had a distressed phone call from Judy to tell us her little son was very ill with a breathing problem. John immediately put him on his absent healing list and I concentrated on sending out psychic energy to make him well. I felt sure it would help and as I hadn't picked up any panic from Judy in the intervening weeks I was certain the boy couldn't be any worse. Nevertheless I didn't *know* and until I received definite news I couldn't fully relax.

Then one afternoon I was doing a sitting for a magazine in Auckland when it started to go wrong. I'd been getting a lot of good evidence and then I seemed to go off beam.

'They're telling me about someone called Sam,' I said.

The reporter shook her head. 'No, I don't know anyone of that name.'

I returned the name for checking. Back it came loud and positive, *Sam*. Still the reporter couldn't accept it. My father's name was Sam, of course, and his warning to me to get down from the dais in the bookshop was still fresh in my mind. Was he trying to get through to me again?

'No, not your father,' Ramanov assured me. And the name came through again.

'Sam,' said a voice. 'Sam's better.'

Totally confused by now, I shook my head. 'I've got my wires crossed somewhere,' I told the reporter. 'I'll have to clear the vibration and start again.'

I blocked my mind to Sam and was about to tune in again, when the phone rang. Saved by the bell, I thought with relief. 'Excuse me a moment,' I apologized and hurried to answer it.

'Hello, Doris!' came a dear, familiar voice over the line. 'It's Judy.'

'Judy! How lovely to hear from you,' I cried with pleasure.

'I won't keep you now because I know you're probably busy,' said Judy. 'I just wanted to let you know that Sam's so much better we thought we'd come over and see you at your hotel.'

I nearly dropped the receiver. We'd found Sam. Grinning, I went through the arrangements with Judy and then returned to my sitting.

'It'll be all right now,' I assured the reporter. 'I've found Sam. We can get on.' And I was right. The sitting went ahead smoothly with no more mysteries.

A few days later Judy and her family drove for three hours to visit us at our hotel in Wellington. They arrived slightly earlier than expected and they got to the room before I did because I'd had to go to the hairdressers. I was staggered when my door was opened by an attractive man I'd never seen before in my life, who proceeded to throw his arms around me and give me a great bear hug. Then Judy pushed him out of the way and hugged me herself and we all squeezed back into the room laughing and weeping a little.

The children were beautiful. Bright, intelligent and full of life, very like their mother. We had tea and sandwiches sent up and while we sat round eating and chattering, Judy began to unpack a big bag she'd brought.

'You sounded so tired on the phone, Doris, I thought you needed something to buck you up,' she explained and out came her herbal remedies and a list of instructions!

Then someone noticed that Trinity had disappeared and the bedroom door was open.

'For God's sake go and see what she's doing,' cried Judy to her husband, but I couldn't resist peeping round the door myself. There was Trinity sitting on the bed, gossiping away to someone on the telephone. She'd dialled a series of numbers at random and managed to get a connection!

We had a very happy afternoon and it was even harder to part this time than it was before, but John and I promised that if we ever get the chance we'll go to stay with them at their home. In the meantime, there are always the letters . . .

Of course I wasn't in New Zealand simply to look up old friends and very soon I was immersed in non-stop work. Again, I seemed to be busy every minute of the day, and only a few of those endless shows and interviews remain in my mind.

I remember doing a phone-in in Auckland, where we were staying in the same villa Yootha Joyce used when she was in New Zealand, when a man came on the line asking if I could help. I promised to do my best. Almost immediately I heard a woman's voice. Her accent sounded a little blurred but I thought she said her name was Maddie.

'Would that be short for Madeleine?' I asked the caller.

'I don't think so, Doris,' said the man. 'The nearest I can get to that name is Maisie.'

'Well, it's a similar sound, she might be saying Maisie,' I said. I asked the woman to give me some more information to establish her identity.

'She's talking about the violent death of a young girl and man,' I went on in surprise.

'Yes, that's right. Maisie is the dead girl's mother,' said the man.

I knew I was on the right track then. 'She says it was to do with a property out in the country,' I continued. 'Who's Alan?'

'I am,' said the man.

'Well, Maisie says don't worry, it wasn't Arthur. Arthur wasn't there. D'you know what she means?'

'Yes, I do,' cried Alan in delight. 'Arthur's my son. His name is Arthur Alan Thomas.'

This meant nothing to me but a gasp went up in the studio. I discovered afterwards that Arthur had been convicted for this crime and although he was later pardoned his father wanted to clear his name beyond all doubt.

Suddenly I could smell a strong animal smell, either sheep or pigs and I was in a room where there had been a terrific struggle. It seemed that I was lying on the floor by the sofa and a young girl was talking to me. She said her name was Jeanette.

'Does the name Jeanette mean anything to you?' I asked Alan.

'Yes,' he said. 'That's the murdered girl.'

Jeanette told me that two men were responsible and they weren't Europeans. One of them wore glasses and they drove a large vehicle, an estate car or a van. It was dark coloured and could have been green or navy blue.

They wanted to be cut in on something, she explained, and when her husband wouldn't agree to it they'd turned on them.

Then in my mind I was going up a narrow rocky path. 'I don't think a vehicle could get up here,' I said. 'It's not wide enough. I don't think even a wheelbarrow could do it but I think that's where they took Jeanette's body.'

Then Maisie came back. 'Tell Arthur we're sorry for all the trouble he's been through,' she said and the vibration faded and she was gone.

It was as if a spell had been broken in the studio. People started whispering and moving about. Alan on the phone was thrilled. His son had been completely exonerated as far as he was concerned. The broadcast also attracted the attention of the police, who apparently recognized much of what I'd said as correct.

I became involved in another murder case quite by chance during a radio show in Wellington. The city was nicknamed Windy Wellington, I was told, because there's always a breeze blowing, but as we drove to the station I thought Windy Wellington with a hard 'i' would be more appropriate because of the winding roads. We wound up and up through green lanes and rolling hills until we finally reached the radio station on the top.

I was supposed to be doing an ordinary interview but half way through Roger, the presenter, suddenly put his hand in his pocket and produced a photograph. 'Can you do anything with that, Doris?'

I looked at it and saw a pretty young girl with wide, clear eyes and shining hair framing her face.

'This girl's missing,' I said.

'That's right,' agreed Roger.

Once more a picture formed in my mind. 'I can see a road with trees lining one side of it and heavy traffic moving along. It must be a main road of some kind,' I said out loud, my ears full of the roar of cars. 'There's a fork in the road, one road bearing to the left and the other going straight on . . .'

Suddenly the picture changed. I was in it myself and I was the young girl. I had a canvas pack on my back and I was inside a vehicle which took the left-hand fork. Then I heard the girl's voice. She told me her name was Mona Blade.

'She says she was on her way home but she never got there,' I said. 'She's written to a girl named Susan.'

Then I was aware of a very deep ravine, damp and rich with vegetation. 'Her pack is down there,' I said, 'and she keeps saying something about a watch. Did you find her watch?'

'No,' said Roger, 'but they found a man's watch.'

Then I mentioned a name and it turned out that this was the name engraved on the back of the watch.

The programme caused a great fuss in the papers and the police inspector working on the case flew to see me because apparently, out of two hundred and seventy–nine miles of motorway, I'd pinpointed the five miles where she was last seen.

Of all the exciting things that happened on our tour I think the most exciting was the Maori welcome I was given at Rotorua Airport. Ken, who was looking after us at this point, warned me about it beforehand and though I didn't know what it involved I was looking forward to it immensely. It was a great honour, Ken explained, normally reserved only for Prime Ministers and royalty and I was thrilled that they were going to all this trouble for me.

The morning arrived, dull and grey but exciting nevertheless. I sat in our hotel room in Auckland waiting for the car that was taking us to the airport. Our bags were packed, I'd swallowed the tiny amount of breakfast that my nervous stomach would allow and we were ready to leave. The phone rang. John leapt to answer it.

'Car's here,' he cried, dropping the receiver.

There was instant bustle. I grabbed my handbag,

jumped to my feet and gasped. The floor swung away from under me and the room spun round. Blindly I groped for something to hang on to and suddenly John was at my side.

'What's the matter? What is it? Here, come on, sit down,' and he guided me back into the chair.

'Oh, no,' I moaned as John fetched a glass of water. It had happened again, the same thing that had happened in Brisbane. Well, I couldn't possibly be ill, not today, not when the Maoris were waiting. Pull yourself together, Doris, I told myself firmly, but my legs were like soft butter and I couldn't stand. I drank the water, crying with frustration.

'Father, Ramanov, *please*,' I begged silently. '*Please* give me the strength to go.'

'You must rest, child,' said Ramanov's voice.

'I know, I know,' I explained, 'but after the Maori welcome. I promise I'll rest then.'

It seemed to me that this internal struggle went on for several minutes. Then the presence of Ramanov and my father receded and my head cleared.

'We should be able to reach them on the phone . . .,' someone was saying . . . 'not too late . . . call it off . . .'

'No!' I cried suddenly. 'Don't call it off. I'm going.'

'But, Doris, you can't,' said John.

'Yes I can,' I insisted. 'If you could just help me down to the car, I can make it.'

'You must see a doctor, love.'

'When we get there, I promise,' I said. 'Look, I'm much better now.'

He wasn't happy about it but he agreed. I was half carried to the car and then practically hoisted on to the plane. Despite my protests I really did feel terribly drained and ill and I collapsed gratefully in the big plane seat. I hardly moved a muscle throughout the journey I was so tired.

It seemed as if I'd only just closed my eyes when the

plane touched down again and we were in Rotorua. An air hostess appeared at my side.

'Mrs Stokes, would you like to get off first, please?'

How sweet of her, I thought, she must be able to see I'm not well. But when I got to the door, I realized that this was all part of the plan. Below me, great shining puddles covered the windswept tarmac, misty grey clouds almost touched the ground and there in front of the plane, shivering in his bare feet and grass skirt was a Maori warrior.

'Hello, Doris,' called one of the ground crew as I walked shakily down the steps. 'Real English weather this. Bet it reminds you of home!'

It did too, and so did the icy cold air. I smiled at the half-naked warrior. Poor man, he must be frozen. He obviously took my smile as the signal that I was ready because at that moment he walked towards me and placed a small chamois leather bag on the ground not far from my feet.

Ken came up behind me. 'Don't touch it yet, Doris,' he whispered. 'I'll tell you when,' and to my astonishment, the warrior started doing a war dance. He leapt about, his long black hair bouncing, his feet nimble on the cold tarmac. He threatened me with his spear, he turned his back on me, then he turned round again, stuck his tongue out as far as it would go and began pulling faces. All the while the rest of the tribe in garlands, grass skirts, bare feet and goose pimples, waited by the terminal building.

The chief performed another energetic dance and then Ken whispered, 'You can pick up your gift now.'

'I daren't!' I whispered back in anguish. 'My head's so dizzy I daren't bend down.'

So Ken bent down, picked it up and put the little bag into my hands. As he did so the whole tribe started waving palm leaves and shouting what sounded like 'Teeckla!': Welcome.

Ken told me the word I should shout back, which I did

and then he said I must go and rub noses twice with each one of them. 'They have welcomed you into their tribe and you have to acknowledge you belong to them.'

So, giggling happily, I went down the line by the terminal door, carefully rubbing noses with each Maori! I wonder if the Queen does this? I thought. It was certainly one of the most extraordinary experiences of my life.

The welcome over, I was whisked away to the hotel where the doctor was waiting. He gave me a thorough examination.

'Well, Mrs Stokes,' he said when he'd finished, 'there's nothing I can do. You are exhausted. You've got to rest, that's all there is to it.'

'Yes, doctor, I will,' I assured him, silently adding – but there won't be much chance today. A press conference had been arranged, I was informed, as we were driving away from the airport and at this very moment the reporters were assembled in the hotel waiting for my appearance. Then later that evening we were to go to an honorary supper laid on by Rotorua Church. After that I'd rest, I promised myself.

To save time at the doctor's, I'd slipped down the shoulder straps of my underskirt instead of undressing completely and after the examination I hastily pulled my dress on again and rushed out to meet the reporters. Half way across the hotel I was suddenly aware that I felt extremely uncomfortable. Something was tight and twisted across my middle and something else was flapping round my legs. I looked down and to my horror saw that my underskirt was hanging out about five inches below my dress. Goodness, what's happened? I wondered. Has something snapped? Then it dawned. In my haste to get away from the doctor, I'd only pulled up one shoulder strap. To sort it out would mean going back to my room, or finding a ladies' room and getting undressed and then dressed all over again.

Oh well, I thought, it's no good worrying now, I'll just

have to get on with it. They can think what they like. And so in I went, my underskirt flapping like a flag.

They couldn't fail to notice, of course, but the reporters were far too polite to say anything and the conference went very smoothly. They certainly couldn't accuse me of putting on airs and graces!

During the conference I couldn't help noticing a Maori vicar enter the room. He didn't look like a journalist to me and I wondered what he wanted. In the end I decided he must simply be curious because he just stood at the back listening quietly and saying nothing. Then to my surprise, when it was over, he came and joined me on the sofa and took hold of my hand.

'Don't you recognize him, Doris?' asked Ken.

'Well, no, I'm afraid I don't,' I admitted a little embarrassed. How could I forget a Maori vicar, for goodness sake? 'Have we met before?'

'He's the warrior who welcomed you at the airport!' chuckled Ken.

'Good heavens!' I exclaimed staring into the beaming face, and when I looked carefully I saw that indeed it was the same man.

I had tea with the vicar and then John led me away for a rest in our room before our special supper.

'I don't think you should go,' John was muttering as I slipped into bed.

'Oh, John,' I said. 'It's too late to cancel it now. They'll have got everything ready. I'll be fine when I've had a sleep.'

It was true. I did feel quite a lot better for my rest and when we arrived at the little hall I was so glad we'd made the effort. Never in my life have I seen such a spread! There was smoked marlin, oysters, trout, sea food, meats and salads of every possible description. They must have spent days preparing the meal.

There were about a hundred people present, many of them children, and they all made a tremendous fuss of me.

The children climbed all over me, the adults tried to tempt me with the very best delicacies from the table and half way through the evening John and I were made honorary members of the church and presented with a diploma which now stands in our hall at home.

At one point a lady came over shyly and touched my arm. 'Doris, my husband doesn't normally hold with this sort of thing but he's seen you on television and read your book and he's made you these.' She put a little case into my hands and when I lifted the lid I found a beautiful brooch with matching ring that this man had made himself.

Before I could find words to thank her, someone else tapped me on the shoulder. 'Look, Doris! Look what they've written on the windows.'

I glanced up and there in the steam on the glass, the children had finger-traced the words, 'We love Granny Doris. Come back soon.' I was absolutely overwhelmed. The party went on around me, the people pressed close but I could hardly see them through my tears. What had I done to deserve so much, I wondered, as I groped for a handkerchief and it was several minutes before I dared speak.

We had to leave quite early since I was still under doctor's orders to rest, but I took away with me memories that I shall treasure forever.

There were still several moving moments to come. The next day I was to give a demonstration at Rotorua Theatre. I walked in and the atmosphere nearly knocked me over it was so powerful. There were eight or nine hundred people present and they had been singing hymns while they waited, which built up the atmosphere marvellously. Then, to my surprise, before I started working, two young girls climbed on to the stage and did a belly dance. The Maori drums were beating and the atmosphere charged and charged until I thought the place would explode. It might not be orthodox, but what did that matter? Living and laughing and loving were surely all that counted. It didn't matter how ill I felt, I knew I couldn't go wrong with a power like this all round me.

There was a short break in the middle of my demonstration and when I started again a man stood up with a bible in his hand and started heckling me.

'Where does God come into all this? That's what I want to know,' he shouted.

This kind of interruption doesn't worry me too much because I know mediums have to expect and be able to answer criticism.

'I always start with a prayer and dedicate my work to God,' I explained. 'I couldn't do my job without God's help.'

'It says in the bible you shouldn't dabble with spirits,' he insisted.

'And it also says in the bible you must test the spirits to see if they are good,' I said, 'and I do.'

The argument went on and even the president's wife joined in to try to explain our point of view. The man wouldn't listen. He was intent on disrupting the meeting, and it was quite clear he didn't genuinely want to know the rights and wrongs of our ideas at all.

This thought must have struck the audience at the same time it struck me because just then, in the middle of another tirade, someone started to boo him. Immediately the jeer was picked up and within seconds nine hundred people had turned on him, booing at the top of their voices. 'We came here to listen to Doris!' someone yelled. 'Let her speak.'

It must have been frightening to be on the wrong side of that crowd and the man hastily sat down, rather wisely I thought, and didn't open his mouth again.

The demonstration continued with the evidence pouring through and when it was over the audience spontaneously jumped to its feet clapping. Someone started singing *Now is the hour for us to say goodbye* and nine hundred voices joined in. The children rushed forward and put their arms round my waist, the words of the song soared until the roof must almost have cracked and a tremendous wave of warmth and love from this great mass of people engulfed me. I just stood there with tears pouring down my face, unable to say a word.

It was very difficult to leave and when I finally did reach the airport, there they were again, lined up on the tarmac with a bouquet of flowers and singing *We'll Meet Again*!

After New Zealand we flew to Tasmania and by this time my impressions were getting very hazy indeed. I had done so much travelling, spoken to so many people, made so many communications, stayed in so many hotel rooms and re-packed our cases so many times that every place was beginning to seem just like the last. Only a few memories stand out. In Tasmania I was struck again by the great beauty and freshness of the country and the way everything was so clean and welcoming.

I can't recall any of my work there except that I did a radio show with a young man called Mike Dodds. Mike was very tongue-in-cheek about the whole thing but after we'd recorded sittings with a few people he'd brought along to the studio, he seemed more impressed and even offered to play a record for me on his early morning breakfast show the next day.

'I'd like one of my favourites by Jim Reeves,' I said eagerly. '*May the Good Lord Bless and Keep You* because it says to everyone what I'd like to say and never have the time.'

'Right,' said Mike, 'I'll see if we've got that in our library.'

The next morning during the breakfast show we were already on the road, heading for the next town on our itinerary.

'Oh, could you put on the radio?' I asked the driver. 'There might be a record for me.'

Sure enough the record library had found my Jim Reeves favourite and I listened to it happily.

Then Mike came on again with great excitement in his voice. 'I've got something very exciting to tell you after the next commercial,' he promised enticingly.

'I wonder what's happened?' remarked John. We speculated over whether Princess Anne might have had another baby, or the Queen announced a visit to Tasmania and then Mike came back and to our surprise started to talk about the sittings I'd recorded the day before.

'The tape went down for processing and when it came back we found that there are other voices on it. Voices you can hear when there was absolute silence in the studio and only Doris and her sitter were speaking. Don't ask me how it happened. We've made exhaustive enquiries. Even if the tape had been used before, we have magnetic cleaning processes so that the tape is wiped completely clean. No old material could remain on it. We can find no explanation for these voices.'

Unfortunately Mike didn't tell us what the voices had said and our car soon moved out of the station's range, so we never did find out. I'd love to know.

My other striking memory of Tasmania is of our hotel room in Hobart. Our hotel was a tall circular building with thirty-six floors and we were given the penthouse suite on the top. When they showed John and I to our room our eyes nearly popped out of our heads. Decorated in red and gold, there was a huge four-poster bed draped with red curtains, pink velvet sofas, a well-stocked bar and pictures of naked ladies on the wall.

It looked out over the sea and it was so high up the tables and chairs in the sea-side garden looked like dolls' furniture set on a postage stamp.

We nicknamed it the Sin Bin, and thought it was a shame to waste it on an old married couple like us!

I did several shows which went off well, and then we flew back to New Zealand where I did a few more. One I recall was held in a basket-ball stadium and as the car drew up outside I couldn't believe my eyes. The queue of people stretched from the entrance right down the road and round the corner. It was cold and pouring with rain but they stood there patiently waiting to get in.

Not for the first time, my legs turned to jelly and my stomach started fluttering. They'd all come to see me. Everything depended on me – but what did they want? What did they expect me to do? If I was able to get messages for twenty or thirty of them I'd be lucky and yet there must be thousands expecting something.

The show was supposed to start at eight but I didn't get on until quarter to nine because they had to put extra seats in to accommodate the crowd and even then three hundred were turned away. When I finally walked a little timidly out into that great arena, such a roar went up that I nearly turned tail and fled.

I'm told the demonstration went well, though my dizzy head came on again and I had to be helped off at the end, the cheering of the crowd ringing in my ears. Backstage the stadium staff presented me with a bouquet of flowers.

'How sweet of you,' I said feeling overwhelmed all over again.

'Well, we want to thank you, Doris,' said the manager. 'We've never had the stadium as full as this.'

My last memory of New Zealand is of waiting at the airport in Auckland for the Australia-bound plane. A young man called Wayne Stevens was looking after us and for some reason I turned to him and asked, 'Have you got a present for your girlfriend, Wayne?'

He looked horrified. 'No! Thank goodness you reminded me, Doris. I'll pop back to the duty free shop. Won't be a minute.'

I dropped into a big, squashy chair in the lounge. Whenever I stopped moving I felt exhausted. Quite honestly I wished I was flying back to Britain and not Australia just then. Not that my love of Australia had diminished, it was simply that I wanted to get back to a permanent bed and a stable routine again after weeks of living like a gypsy.

The minutes ticked by and I glanced round wondering where Wayne had got to. It was then that I noticed the policeman enter the lounge, dressed in a similar uniform to our bobbies at home, but with a white helmet in place of our traditional blue. He wandered between the seats staring into faces as if he was looking for someone and eventually he reached me.

'Doris Stokes?' he demanded.

I stared up at six feet of sombre blue and my heart turned over. I thought we were going to be arrested. What had we done? Was some document not in order?

I heard a commotion behind me and turned to see Wayne Stevens dashing across from the duty free shop crying, 'What's the matter? What's the matter?'

The policeman ignored him. Taking off his helmet he knelt down by my side.

'I just want to say thank you, Doris, for coming to New Zealand. I was at your show last night and I thought it was marvellous.' And while I was still speechless with shock, he leant down, kissed me on the cheek, stood up, replaced his helmet and strode quickly away.

'What was that all about? What did you do?' asked Wayne reaching us breathlessly.

But I didn't answer. A pink blush was spreading warmly over my cheeks and I could feel my face breaking into a silly grin.

'Well!' was all I could say.

The excitement still wasn't over. When I arrived in Australia I walked right back into controversy. I was still under doctor's orders to rest because on top of my other problem, which was eventually diagnosed as a slight stroke, I managed to catch a particularly nasty form of gastric 'flu which also felled the All Blacks rugby team.

One morning I was having a late breakfast. I had no

plans for the day ahead, and decided I would spend my time flopping about and sleeping. I thought it would be nice to listen to Bert Newton on the radio while I had my breakfast, so I switched it on. I was very glad I did.

Soon I was listening to Bert's guest of the day, a Mr James Randi, a magician whose mission, he said, was to expose fakes like Uri Geller and Doris Stokes. He could duplicate Geller's spoon bending by normal magic tricks, he claimed, and as for me, I was taking the Australian people for a ride. He had seen me in London and I was no good then and I was no good now.

I crashed my cup back on its saucer in anger. Randi? James Randi? I was particularly certain that no one of that name had ever been to me for a sitting in London. I don't remember every sitter, of course, but his voice wasn't remotely familiar. Well, he wasn't going to get away with that!

Furiously I pushed back my chair.

'What are you doing now?' asked John looking at my red face.

'I'm not putting up with this, John – it's not true what he's saying!' I strode to the phone and angrily dialling the radio station I got through to Peter, the producer of Bert's show.

'Peter, it's Doris Stokes here. I've just been listening to Mr Randi and I want to answer him. Will you put me on the air?'

Peter put me on the air.

'Now, Mr Randi,' I said. 'I might not be there in body but I'm there in spirit. You can say to me what you have to say.'

It must have been quite a shock for him but he recovered quickly. 'Yes, all right,' he said. 'You're conning the people of Australia.'

I struggled to keep my temper. 'You are saying the Australian people are fools, then?'

'No, I didn't say that,' he replied.

'By implication you did,' I insisted, 'because I was here in 1978 and I am back again now, so if I'm conning the people they must be a pack of fools to be taken in twice.'

He huffed and puffed at this and muttered that that wasn't the point in any case.

'Look, there's a quick way out of this, Mr Randi,' I said. 'You say I'm a fake. Well, if I'm a fake it's possible to duplicate what I do. Now, I'm doing a public meeting on Thursday evening at Dallasbrook Hall so I challenge you to come on stage with me and I'll do my thing with the audience – faking, you call it – and then you fake it in the same way and we'll let the audience make up their own minds.'

'Oh no, I have more important things to do,' replied Mr Randi, rather lamely, I thought, but then I'm biased!

'But you said you wanted to expose fakes!' I pointed out. 'Surely there's nothing more important than that? And by the way, when did you say you saw me in London?'

There was a slight pause. 'January,' he said guardedly.

'January this year?' I queried sweetly.

'That's right,' he said.

I must confess to an unworthy feeling of delight. That was the month I had my hysterectomy operation and the only people I gave sittings to, and even then right at the end of January, were a couple of journalists who couldn't see me at any other time.

'Well, it must have been my spirit body you saw then, son,' I said, 'because I was in hospital having a major operation and I've got documents to prove it.'

Mr Randi struggled on valiantly but I think he knew he was beaten.

'Look,' I said more kindly, 'I believe you're a very good magician, I've never seen you perform but I wouldn't dream of coming on to your show and trying to dissect what you're doing because I don't know anything about it. So what gives you the right to try to dissect what I'm doing when *you* know nothing about it?'

'Oh dear, is that the time?' said Mr Randi. 'I'd love to go on but I've got another appointment and my taxi's ticking away outside.'

And he left abruptly.

That was the last I'd hear of Mr Randi, I thought, but I was wrong. A few days later I stepped off a plane in Brisbane to find television cameras waiting and a knot of reporters who rushed forward the moment I walked through the barrier.

'What do you think about your friend Don Lane?' they asked.

'Why? What's the matter with Don?' I asked in alarm. I hadn't picked up any message that he was ill or had had an accident, but I'd been so tired lately I might have missed it.

'He marched off the set last night,' they said. 'He swore at Mr Randi, swept all his props on to the floor and stormed off. Now he's in trouble with the IBA.'

I was horrified. I had a nasty feeling this was something to do with me.

'Well, I'm very sorry if Don's in trouble,' I said. 'But Don's straight. He must have had a reason for doing it. This man must have said something he couldn't accept. And talking of Mr Randi, let me issue my challenge again. Mr Randi, wherever you are – I'm appearing at such and such a place – come along. Show me up, and if the Australian people boo me off the stage when you've done it I promise I'll go home and never set foot in Australia again!'

This seemed to satisfy the reporters and when we got to our hotel I discovered the airport interview was shown on the six-thirty news and the place was buzzing with the Don Lane Scandal.

Apparently James Randi had appeared on the show and upset Don by implying, or so Don thought, that I was a liar. Don had issued a four-letter word and stormed off. It was the four-letter word which angered the IBA more than the storming off.

I was terribly worried. Suppose poor Don got the sack. It was largely my fault. If I hadn't retaliated so angrily when Mr Randi spoke on the radio, perhaps he would have been forgotten. Maybe I should have kept quiet and let people believe what they wanted to believe.

I was still turning this over in my mind when Don rang. He had heard I was worried and wanted to set my mind at rest.

'What's up, kid?' he asked cheerfully when I came to the phone.

'Oh, Don, I've been so worried,' I said. 'What with this Mr Randi and the IBA. They said you were in terrible trouble.'

'Now, look, don't you worry about me. I can take care of myself,' he said kindly. 'I've been on the air and apologized to the viewers for that word I used but no way will I apologize to that man unless he can bring me documents or proof that the things he says about people are true.'

'But what about the IBA?'

'I've squared it with them now. They're satisfied with the apology for the four-letter word.'

'Oh, thank goodness for that,' I said in relief and made a mental note to take it as a lesson not to be so hasty in future.

I suppose I did get a lot of mileage out of the James Randi episode, however. He never did take up my challenge to share the stage with me at a public meeting but after that, whenever I appeared anywhere I always started by saying, 'Hello everybody. Where's Mr Randi, then?' and everyone would fall about laughing. At one place a man shouted back, 'If he turns up here we'll lynch him.' So perhaps it was just as well he stayed away.

At last in mid-August the tour ended and it was time to go home. I was sorry to be saying goodbye to so many friends and to a country that has always felt like home to me, but at the same time I was relieved to be able to step off the merry-go-round for a while.

My last memory of the tour is of leaving Perth and being invited up to the flight deck to meet the captain.

'It's all right,' the captain was saying as I squeezed into the glass-ringed cockpit with what looked like great banks of computers on every side. 'Doris is on board, so I know we'll get there!'

He turned and grinned at me. 'Well, it's a bit of a cheek coming on to my aircraft with a Qantas badge on your lapel!'

I looked down at my collar and blushed. During the outward flight with Qantas they'd presented me with a little gold kangaroo badge and the New Zealand Airways had given me a silver kiwi. I'd forgotten to remove them from my coat.

'Well I haven't got anything from British Airways,' I pointed out reasonably.

So he duly presented me with a set of wings, and I finally stepped on to British soil, wearing my British Airways badge!

CHAPTER 11

'Hello, Mrs Finch – do come in and sit down.'

So this was Mrs Finch. I had spoken to her on the phone, autographed a book for her, but until now I'd never met her. She walked into the flat, a slender, striking woman with delicate bone structure and sleek fair hair brushed back from her face. She perched elegantly on the edge of one of our high-backed armchairs and crossed her long, slim legs.

'Please call me Yolande,' she said.

She looks like a film star, I thought, taking in the expensive well-cut clothes, the good jewellery and the graceful way she moved. Yet I didn't recognize her from any film I'd ever seen and her low voice with its trace of a South African accent wasn't familiar.

Even then I didn't connect her with Peter Finch, the world famous actor who passed over a few years ago – after all Finch is a common name. It wasn't until one of the most vivid sittings I've ever done, including some of the saltiest language I've come across, was under way, that I realized whom I was talking to.

It was October by now, nearly two months since I'd returned from Australia and once again I was supposed to be resting. I was so tired I'd fallen victim to just about every cold and bug around and apart from attending a wonderful welcome home party thrown for me by Wimbledon Church, I'd done very little.

It was strange how Yolande Finch came to have a sitting with me. On the way back from a radio interview about her new book, *Finchy*, on the subject of life with her ex-husband, she discovered that Eddie, the driver of her car, had also driven me a few times. Eddie was listening to a psychic programme on the radio and Yolande thought it was rubbish.

'Switch that off. It's a load of old nonsense,' she said.

Eddie obligingly turned it off but disagreed that the subject was nonsense and proceeded to tell Yolande about me and how I'd once given him an impromptu sitting as we were driving along the road.

'She's written a book 'an all,' Eddie added. 'I'll get you a copy. Then you can see for yourself.'

Yolande thought no more about it and the first I heard of it was when Eddie drove me to Covent Garden for some function and asked if I would autograph a copy of *Voices* for him. 'Yes, of course, Eddie. Who's it for?' I asked as I knew he'd already read it.

'Mrs Finch,' he replied. So I quickly scribbled, 'For Mrs Finch, God bless, Mrs Doris Stokes', thinking no more about it than if I'd written for Mrs Smith or Mrs Brown.

Both Yolande and her daughter Samantha read the book and in the end Samantha, anxious to know more about her father, begged her mother to contact me. I was still supposed to be resting, of course, but there was something about this Mrs Finch's voice that made me disregard the doctor's orders. Normally I only did this for women who'd lost children, but something made me say yes to Mrs Finch. It was as if it had cost her a lot to bring herself to phone me and I felt it would be wrong to dash her hopes now.

I tuned in and immediately a strong male voice was there. He said his name was Peter. 'I passed with a coronary,' he said. His manner was forceful, even arrogant and there was something familiar about his voice. The next second it clicked: this must be *the* Peter Finch, the film star.

'It was a terrible mistake to let you divorce me,' he told Yolande. 'You were the one who wanted the divorce, not me. We should have worked things out. It would have been my salvation.'

'In what way? Why would it have been your salvation?'
I asked.

'I used to get very worried and frightened,' said Peter.
'I was at the top but there was always the fear of slipping.
Drink was the only way I could cope, so I turned to the
bottle. I didn't realize what it was doing to me. I used to
get drunk because I was frightened. I used to live for the
drinks cabinet, but I was too young to die. I was only
sixty-two.'

At that, another voice chimed in. 'You're lucky. I was
only *fifty*-two.'

'Who's that?' I asked. This sitting was beginning to get
out of hand.

'Thomas,' replied the man crisply.

'That's my father,' said Yolande in surprise.

'I passed with a coronary just as Peter did,' Thomas
explained and would have said more but I got the
impression that Peter was elbowing him out of the way.

'I married again after Yolande,' he said, 'and there was
another child. Diane.'

Yolande agreed that this was true.

Then a woman's voice pushed in and gave me five names
one after the other: 'Sophia, Antonia, Francis, Gertrude
and Rose,' she announced, triumphant at having made
herself heard above the men.

I was beginning to feel as if my head was a football they
were kicking around between them. 'One at a time, please.
I can only talk to one of you at a time.' Wearily I repeated
the names but Yolande shook her head.

'No, I'm sorry they mean nothing to me.'

'She doesn't know what you mean, dear,' I told the
woman.

'Yes she does,' she insisted and repeated the names
again. 'And Girly tells me to tell you she gave you her pin.'

Yolande looked completely mystified by this piece of
information and I could tell by the look on her face that
she was wondering whether I was some kind of crank.

My spirit contact was still quite confident that she was talking to the right person, however. I must be the one that's wrong then, I thought. Have I got the message right, dear? I asked silently. Girly gave Yolande her pin?

'I didn't say *pin*,' scoffed the woman in a strong South African accent. 'I said *pen*.'

'I'm sorry, Yolande, I got that wrong,' I said. 'It should have been pen, not pin.'

At once a great smile lightened Yolande's face. 'Oh, of course! It's my Great-Aunt Girly. Her name is Gertrude, Doris, but everyone called her Girly. She gave me her pen the day before she died. She was ninety-seven and she only went three months ago.'

Yolande could hardly sit still for excitement now. Leaning forward, eyes blazing, she suddenly recalled that Sophia, Antonia, Francis and Rose were Girly's dead sisters. In fact, Rose was her grandmother.

Then Peter's voice came back, still obviously on the subject of Yolande.

'She was my lover, mistress, wife and friend,' he said. Then he added with a laugh in his voice, 'She used to nag me though.'

'I only nagged you for your own good,' Yolande retorted, stung.

That did it.

'Well, I didn't ask for the bloody divorce, did I!' Peter snapped back and before I realized it we were in the middle of a flaming row. They both seemed to forget I was there and started shouting at each other. At one point Peter's language got so strong I had to ask him to modify it.

'You tell me exactly what he's saying,' cried Yolande angrily.

Peter mentioned his daughter by the nickname that only he used, Sam, and he also talked of his son, Charles.

'Well, why didn't you provide for them if you were so fond of them?' snapped Yolande.

'I did,' Peter protested. 'I made special provision for them in my will – but you know what I'm like with paper work. I didn't realize that by remarrying it was automatically annulled.'

Yolande sighed. 'I know, I know.'

'Accountant, accountant, get an accountant,' Peter went on.

This amazed Yolande bacause during his life on earth Peter wouldn't hear of accountants. Then she remembered that in order to come to see me she had cancelled an appointment with her accountant.

Things calmed down after that, I was relieved to find, and the sitting ended with Peter expressing his love for his family and his regret that they hadn't managed to work things out in their marriage.

'D'you know, Doris,' said Yolande just before she left, 'while I was writing my book I had the strangest feeling that Finchy was there by my elbow. I thought it was just my imagination at the time but now I'm not so sure. What do you think?'

'I think he was there, Yo,' I told her positively. 'I'm sure he was.'

This wasn't the first time I'd talked to a famous person without realizing who they were. Some years before a young man had telephoned to ask if I could help him. He and a young colleague were writing a book and wanted to contact a pop star called Buddy Holly. I'm ashamed to say that I hadn't heard of this particular singer, but I explained, as I always do, that you can't just nominate whom you'd like to speak to. A lot of people would love to have a chat with Sir Winston Churchill or President Kennedy or Elvis Presley, but they won't come back to a complete stranger. Why should they?

The young man said he understood this but as he thought he had a slight connection with the singer, he'd still like me to have a go.

'All right, son,' I agreed. 'But I can't promise anything.'

Anyway, the sitting started and as I'd feared this Buddy Holly didn't come. Instead I found myself talking to a young man named Charles Hardy something – I couldn't catch the last part of his name. He told me his wife's name and explained that he'd been killed in a plane crash. He also named the people who had been with him in the plane. I asked him what he looked like and in reply I felt him put a huge pair of spectacles on my face.

'He wore glasses,' I explained to the two young men, 'and they were very important to his appearance. He feels that you'll recognize him by the glasses. They were very large.'

Finally William said, 'Paul is buying my music.'

'Paul who?' I asked.

'Paul Mac . . .' The end of the name was so fuzzy I couldn't make it out.

'Sorry, love, I didn't catch that,' I apologized.

William tried again but it was no use. I couldn't get it. 'He will be on the television,' William promised at last, 'and then you will know who I'm talking about.'

It was the end of the sitting and I was rather dissatisfied. 'I'm sorry I didn't get the person you wanted,' I apologized to the boys. 'I did warn you.'

'But you did,' they assured me. 'That was him; Charles Hardy, that was Buddy Holly!'

And two days later I was watching the news when a picture of Paul McCartney flashed on to the screen with the announcement that he was hoping to buy some of Holly's music.

My sittings continued erratically throughout the winter, because there were some people I just couldn't turn away no matter what the doctor said.

I remember one couple, Stan and Jackie Ross – how could I tell them I was too tired when they didn't know which way to turn because they had lost their beloved son, Daniel?

During the sitting, little Daniel wanted to tell me about

his funeral and he kept drawing something in the air. At first I thought it was an engine, but it had a handle and it was made of flowers. I was absolutely stumped.

'I'm sorry,' I apologized. 'He's showing me this shape,' and I traced it in the air, the way Daniel had done, 'and he says it's made of flowers. I can't think what it can be.'

Then his parents suddenly clasped their hands in joy. 'It's a lawnmower, Doris,' they cried.

Apparently Daniel used to love to mow the lawn and so they had had a wreath made up in the shape of a lawnmower as the centre piece of his funeral flowers.

They were very nice people indeed. A few days later they sent me a photograph of Daniel, to put with my other spirit children, accompanied by a letter and two beautiful bunches of roses – one for me and one for the spirit children because they had noticed the flower beside each photograph. I'm sure the children knew, because I explained it to them as I put the fresh flowers beside each picture.

'Aren't these roses lovely, Daniel?' I explained, placing his in water first because they were from his parents. 'They're from your mummy and daddy for you, and all the other children you've met on the other side.' And he seemed to smile back at me from his photograph, as if he was very pleased with them.

It is heartrending to lose a child and of all the ways a child can go, suicide is the hardest for the parents to take. They torment themselves with guilt and grief and in many cases they never get over the cruel blow. Their lives are ruined forever. So when, shortly after the Ross' sitting, I received a desperate letter from a couple whose fifteen-year-old daughter had apparently committed suicide, I knew I would have to see them at once.

They arrived one afternoon, a small pretty woman with clouds of soft dark hair and a haunted, silent man with deep blue eyes. Apprehension and scepticism rose from him like steam from a wet coat, and I knew I would have to treat him carefully.

'Would you like a drink?' I asked, thinking it might help them to relax.

'No, thank you,' said the man stiffly. 'We stopped at a cafe on the way.'

They lapsed into silence again. It was clear I couldn't ease them into the sitting. I'd just have to begin at once. I tuned in and straight away a young, girlish voice was chatting excitedly.

'I'm Linda,' she told me, 'and that's my mummy and daddy.'

'Can you give me their names, Linda?' I asked.

'My daddy's name is Ray,' she said and there was a long pause. 'Mummy's name begins with three letters,' she said at last, a little reluctantly. 'It's a Pa sound.'

'Is it Pam?' I asked going along with the little game.

'No,' said Linda.

'Then if it isn't Pam, it must be Pat,' I guessed.

'That's it, that's right,' Linda laughed. 'It's Pat.'

I asked how old she was when she passed. 'Fifteen and a half,' she told me and as she came closer I felt she had long dark hair swinging round her shoulders and she was a pretty girl, very like her mother.

At the mention of her passing, Linda's voice changed and became upset.

'Can you ever forgive me? Can you ever forgive me?' she cried miserably.

'Will you ever forgive us?' asked Ray, his voice breaking.

'What happened, Linda,' I asked gently.

'There was a boy,' she sniffed. 'He was older than me.'

'Was there something you were afraid of? Did you think you were pregnant?' I probed gently.

She got very annoyed at that suggestion. 'Indeed I wasn't pregnant,' she said indignantly.

'Well, what happened, then?' I persisted, and gradually the whole sad story came out. She was involved with a boy of nineteen and her parents disapproved. They weren't very keen on the boy and they thought he was too old for her. They pressured Linda to give him up. He was possessive and pressured her to stay with him and at fifteen it was too much for her to cope with. As well as this she was jealous of her younger brother, Martin. Martin suffered from asthma and needed a lot of attention. In her depressed state, Linda thought her brother received all her parents' love and she received none.

'I was all mixed up,' she said to her parents. 'You were so busy with your own lives I wanted to scare you. You hurt me so much over the boy, I wanted to hurt you back and I wanted everything to be all right again as well, so I took Mummy's pills.

'What a fool I was. I realize now that you loved me after all. Oh, please forgive me.'

She went on to mention that July and October were two important anniversaries. In July Linda had died and as for October:

'Happy birthday, Daddy,' she said.

'There'll be no more birthdays, now,' said Ray bitterly.

At his words Linda burst into tears.

'Tell him he must go forward, Doris,' she begged. 'And he mustn't blame Mum as he has done.'

Reluctantly, with tears in their eyes, Ray and Pat admitted that they hadn't been speaking. Ray blamed Pat for leaving her pills lying around and pressuring Linda, and Pat blamed Ray for going on at Linda so often. They promised to try to be more understanding with each other.

'I'm so glad,' said Linda more happily. 'It feels as if a great weight has been lifted from me.'

She went on to talk about Dr Harrison and added that John had been with him. Ray and Pat looked at each other blankly.

'Dr Harrison?' said Pat. 'I don't think she knew a Dr Harrison. That's not our GP's name.'

But they discovered later that Dr Harrison was the pathologist who was called in to perform the autopsy on Linda's body and the mortician who assisted him was called John. Apparently Pat had kept going to the mortuary and begging the mortician to be gentle with her daughter's body. It reduced him to tears.

'I'm glad the inquest wasn't what Mummy was worried about,' Linda said and Pat took this to mean that the verdict of the inquest turned out to be accidental death and not suicide as they'd feared.

'I was afraid people would think I'd committed suicide,' Linda went on. 'Well, I didn't. When I went into the bathroom and took the pills I wanted to make myself ill to hurt Mummy and Daddy, that's all. But by the time they reached me it was too late.'

Linda went on to give much more evidence. She named Beaty and Cathy, two girls she had worked with on her Saturday job. She said her mother had started wearing her blue nightdress which used to belong to her and she also described the blue cardigan her mother wore.

At the end of the sitting Ray and Pat were very quiet, almost dazed. They went away thoughtfully and, feeling rather drained, I went to the kitchen to start the dinner. I was peeling onions when suddenly the doorbell rang. I glanced up at the clock. It was four-thirty. Who could it be at this time of day? Terry wasn't due home from work for a couple of hours yet.

Then I heard Linda's voice again. 'It's flowers from Daddy!' she whispered.

Drying my hands on my apron I hurried to the door, but Ray had already gone. There on the doorstep were eighteen long-stemmed carnations and on the card that accompanied them Ray had written, 'Dear Doris, thank you for the hope and strength you have given us.'

CHAPTER 12

Since my last book came out, I've received many readers' letters saying how much they enjoyed the philosophy I talked of and expressing an interest to know more. Well I'm not an intellectual and there are many good books available that explain philosophy far better than I could ever hope to. All I can do is talk of the things that have happened in my life and the lessons that Ramanov has taught me.

Sometimes, when I've been agonizing over some difficult philosophical point Ramanov has interrupted with: 'Look, it doesn't matter how much you philosophize and how many hymns you sing, when you come over here what is inside you will show on the outside. It's what you do and what you are that counts.'

So I try to live my life the way Ramanov and my relatives on the other side would like me to because I don't want them to be ashamed of me when I get there, and I leave the finer points of philosophy to the experts.

If I'm in any doubt as to how I should behave, I think of a story that Estell Roberts, a very famous medium before she passed over, used to tell. It came, she said, from her guide, Red Cloud, and I've never forgotten it. It goes like this:

Once there was a lady who owned a big mansion with the most wonderful gardens. So beautiful were these gardens that people used to come from miles around to look at them. Yet she only had one gardener, a man called Joe, but he so loved this garden that he worked on it from dawn till dusk.

Joe lived in a broken-down cottage on the edge of the estate but he never complained or demanded anything else and he was nearer to God than anyone.

Eventually the time came when Joe had to take his transition and afterwards, no matter how many experts and landscape gardeners the lady employed, the gardens never looked the same again because they weren't tended with love as Joe had tended them.

The time came for the lady to go over. When the guide took her there, she was amazed to find her mansion and gardens, just as beautiful as they had been when Joe had tended them. The estate was just the same, right down to the broken-down cottage where Joe used to live.

'How marvellous!' said the lady in delight. 'It's just like it was on the earth plane.'

And the guide said, 'I'm afraid not. Joe lives in the mansion now because he has earned the right to be there. It is your turn to live in the cottage and when you learn to give in love and self sacrifice, as Joe did, then maybe one day you will earn the right to get your mansion back.'

It's not easy to live like that, of course. I do my best but I'm only human and I fail more often than I succeed: I get bad tempered, I complain, and I forget how very lucky I am. But the funny thing is, the lessons are all around us if only we'd recognize them for what they are.

I was reminded of this very forcibly one day when I was convalescing after my mastectomy operation. I wanted to go home but the doctor, knowing what I was like, thought I'd have a better chance of resting if I spent a few days in a convalescent home. I wasn't at all happy about this, and one morning I'd got up to find it was pouring with rain, our breakfast wasn't ready and my plan to go to the hairdressers would have to be cancelled because a new hairdo would be ruined if I went out in such weather.

I stood in the queue outside the dining-room glowering at the window. The beautiful scenery had disappeared under porridgy cloud; sheets of rain were slapping against the glass and bouncing off the path and great brown puddles were appearing on the sodden lawn. The damp weather made my chest ache more than ever and depression heavier than the cloud outside sank over me.

No one was in more pain than I was, I decided; no one was as miserable as I was. I wanted to go home and I didn't care if I had to leave in a dustcart; I wasn't staying in this gloomy place a day longer.

'Doris Stokes? It is Doris Stokes, isn't it?' asked a timid voice behind me. I scowled at the dissolving garden and didn't turn round. The last thing I felt like was getting involved in small talk. Couldn't she see I was ill?

'Yes, it is,' I said ungraciously.

'I thought it was. Is it raining very hard?'

'Absolutely bucketing down,' I snapped bitterly, hoping to discourage further conversation – particularly conversation of this painfully obvious kind. You only had to glance out of the window to see how hard it was raining.

'Oh, what a shame for you,' the woman persisted. 'Aren't I lucky, I see only what I want to see, so for me it's a lovely, bright day out there.'

At this extraordinary piece of logic I turned round and to my shame I found I was looking at a bent old lady, painfully holding herself upright on two sticks. There were callipers on her legs and as she smiled vaguely somewhere to the right of my shoulder, I realized that she was completely blind.

Remorse shot through me like a physical pain. How could I have been so unkind?

'But you're blind, dear,' I said gently.

'Oh, yes, but I used to have sight,' she explained cheerfully 'and because of that I have lots of beautiful memories. So, now, whatever the weather, I can look at what I choose. I think that's very lucky, don't you?'

I stared at her and a lump came into my throat. 'Yes, dear, I do,' I said humbly.

They say there is always someone worse off than yourself and it's easy to be smug about such clichés. But I've found that clichés are usually clichés because they are true. There

I was, feeling sorry for myself, and that poor, blind, old lady shamed me into realizing that not only was there someone worse off than myself but that she was coping with her severe problems much better than I was with my comparatively minor ones. I was also forced to admit that once again I'd forgotten all Ramanov's teachings about giving out love and friendship because I had been so selfishly wrapped up in my own exaggerated suffering.

I'd failed once again. On the other hand, Ramanov always tells me not to feel too bad about failure. As I explained in my last book, he once explained, 'Failure is not falling down. It's failing to get up when you've fallen down.' I took this to mean that it's how you use your failure that counts. If you learn by a mistake and consciously try not to make it again, then you are progressing and that's the most important thing.

Ramanov has always told me to trust and then everything will work out well. Again this is difficult for me to do, particularly as I'm a natural worrier – if I haven't got something to worry about, I'm worried! Yet time and time again he's helped me out of a difficult situation.

When we were still living in Lancaster we had a desperate phone call from Tony Scott, a comedian friend. He was in a terrible state.

'Doris, please help me,' he begged.

'What's the matter, Tony, you sound awful?' I said anxiously.

'My mother's dying,' Tony explained, his voice choked, 'and she's so frightened. I don't know what to say to her, Doris. Please tell we what to say.'

My mind went blank. This wasn't the sort of work I was used to. What could I suggest? Tony needed an answer quickly, but it was a bit late to try to explain spiritualist philosophy to a woman who was on her death-bed. My thoughts raced round, tangling and going nowhere. Then above my confusion I heard Ramanov's calm voice reciting a poem.

'Tony, have you got a pen? Write this down quickly,' I instructed. And I repeated the words of the poem as Ramanov spoke them:

> 'Gentle spirit, please to come,
>   My life on earth is almost done.
>   Appear before my closing eye,
>   Tell me again I cannot die.
>   Here is my hand, please hold it fast,
>   Then with courage I will pass
>   Across that bridge that's built with love,
>   Into the summer land above.'

Ramanov's voice stopped. 'That's it, Tony. What d'you think?'

There was a pause as Tony read it through. 'It sounds beautiful.'

'Well, read it to your mother and let's hope it helps,' I said.

Half an hour later Tony rang again.

'Bless you, Doris, bless you,' he said, his voice husky. 'My mother's gone and the last thing she said was, "read it again, Tony, read it again!" '

I don't know why I still find it so difficult to trust because Ramanov has been proved right time and time again. On another occasion I was doing a phone-in programme for Monty Moddlin of LBC radio. It was my fourth appearance on the show and Monty explained that he'd received so many letters from people without phones complaining that they were deprived of a chance to talk to me that he had decided to offer mini-sittings to the first six people who reached the studios. What did I think of the idea?

'It's all right with me, Monty,' I said, 'as long as you don't get complaints from the listeners who live too far from the studios!'

Monty laughed. 'Oh, well, I can't think of everything,' and he announced the scheme over the air.

It looked as if it would be a success. The first woman arrived within minutes. The sitting went smoothly and we'd hardly finished when they told me the next sitter was waiting outside.

I took a deep breath. 'Okay, send her in,' I said.

The door opened and I was amazed to see two men whom I recognized. One, a great tall figure with a mexican moustache, long hair and a gold chain round his neck, swept in with a sheaf of papers under his arm. It was Gerald Flemming, a man dedicated to exposing fraudulent mediums. Behind him was Wally Glower, a small, timid looking man who had had a sitting with me some months before.

'You want to talk to Doris?' asked Monty, a little taken aback by their purposeful entrance.

'No,' said Flemming. 'I've come to tell you she's a fraud.' I just sighed but Monty nearly dropped his headphones. This wasn't what he'd had in mind at all!

Quietly I stood up. 'I'm not brawling with him over the air, Monty,' I said. 'I'll leave.'

'You see,' said Flemming triumphantly, 'this is what happens when you face them with it. They run away.'

That did it! Furiously I crashed back into my seat.

'Mr Flemming,' I cried, struggling to keep my temper, 'I wouldn't run away from you in a million years. Now, let's hear what you have to say.'

So he began his tirade. I was chased out of Australia in 1978 by the police, he told the listeners. I couldn't hold my tongue at that.

'Then it's very strange that I'm going back again in July, isn't it?' I pointed out.

'I don't think so,' said Flemming. 'I'm certain you're not.' Well, of course I did go that July.

Then he introduced Wally who would talk about the sitting he'd had with me, Flemming promised, and he proceeded to feed Wally with questions. My heart sank as I listened. I speak to so many people over the years that I can't possibly remember the details of every sitting. It's only the unusual ones that stand out in my mind. I was sure Wally had had a successful sitting but, as I couldn't remember it, I couldn't refute what he was saying.

He claimed that I'd told him all sorts of things that were incorrect and had also warned him not to get married. Monty looked at me, his eyebrows raised, but I couldn't answer. I was sure it wasn't true but how could I deny it when I couldn't recall the occasion?

In the end, Monty got fed up with both of them. 'Okay, you've had your say, gentlemen, now will you leave the studio?'

Satisfied, the two men stood up and as they crossed to the door I caught Wally's eye.

'Wally, I hope you can sleep at night,' I said to him quietly. His face reddened, he dropped his eyes and hurried out.

'Are you all right, Doris?' Monty asked, as soon as the door closed behind them. 'Has it shaken you? Will you go on or do you want to call it a day?'

'No, it's all right, Monty. I'll go on,' I assured him and the programme continued without further interruption.

But the incident did shake me, much more than I cared to admit. I had to fight to keep my voice calm as my stomach churned over and over. I don't mind criticism. If I stand up in public I have to expect public knocks. I've never pretended that I don't make mistakes now and again and I'm willing to own up to them, but the thought that someone to whom I'd never done any harm should come along and tell lies about me was like a physical blow. Why on earth had he done it? Did he hate me that much?

That night, upset and sickened, I turned to Ramanov hoping for some words of comfort.

'Trust,' he said serenely. 'It will be all right.'

But I didn't feel reassured. The damage was done now,

it was too late to undo it. How could everything be all right?

But the months went by and gradually the incident faded from my mind. My work went on as before, no one appeared put off by the remarks and I received several letters of support. I must be prepared for that sort of thing, I told myself. Somehow I must make myself tougher.

I became busier than ever and in the end I'd almost forgotten the whole thing. Then one day, about a year later, I received a letter from Wally. He hadn't been able to sleep at nights, he wrote, and he wanted to ask my forgiveness and to put the record straight. He had told lies, he admitted. He realized now what a rotten thing he had done, particularly as I'd never done anything to hurt him. On the contrary, I had given him a marvellous sitting, even predicting that he would get married and be very happy – which eventually came true. He had also sent copies of this letter to LBC radio and the Psychic News, he explained, in the hope that this would repair any damage his lies had caused.

I read the confession with a glow of pleasure. Of course I forgave Wally, but most important of all Ramanov had been right. I should never have doubted him in the first place.

As I've said before Ramanov has been proved right over and over again. Whenever I worry about bills and rising prices and wonder where the money's going to come from, he has always reminded me to trust, to do my job to the best of my ability and the spirit world will see that I'll never go without. This has always been the case, not only in my life but in other people's.

Phil Edwards, in whose house I saw the baker, attended my teaching class at one time and I told him that he had a marvellous healing power and should use it. Now, Phil was an intelligent, down-to-earth businessman and he wasn't convinced at first, but as more and more people told him the same thing he decided he ought to take it seriously. He was working very hard at the time on his successful garage business but he began to get an increasingly strong feeling that the 'Guvnor', as he calls God, wanted him to devote himself to healing.

The next thing I heard, he had suddenly turned his business over to his son and built a sanctuary with his own hands in the grounds of his beautiful old house in Sussex.

He was soon doing some wonderful healing, but he also had a large family to support and without the money from the garage business, he found it difficult to make ends meet. He was quite convinced, however, that he was doing what his 'Guvnor' wanted him to do and with his wife Sue's encouragement he continued with his work.

Then one day a strange man turned up on the doorstep and Sue thought it must be the tax inspector, but he showed her his card and it turned out he was from the Football Pools. When Phil left the garage Sue had continued to pay their stake in the garage pool's syndicate and now they had had a win. The eight of them would share over a million pounds of prize money the man explained.

It was the answer to all their problems! Phil was able to invest the money and the interest gained replaced the money he used to take out of the business for living expenses. As Phil says, the Guvnor's treated him right.

He treats me right, too. I mentioned earlier that my hysterectomy operation was very expensive and though John and I had a bit put by for new furniture when we moved flats we didn't know whether it was going to be enough. Then one evening, when I was still in hospital recovering from the operation, a nurse came in with an envelope.

'A lady left this for you at reception, Mrs Stokes,' she said. 'We asked if she would like to come in but she said, no, she wouldn't disturb you, and she wouldn't leave a name either. She just put the envelope down and went straight out again.'

'What did she look like?' I asked, my curiosity aroused.

'Well, the receptionist said she was elderly, that's all. She can't remember much about her.'

It could have been anyone, I thought.

'You open it, John,' I said. I was eager to see inside but I was still too weak to lift anything unnecessarily. So John tore across the top of the envelope, pulled out a fat get-well card, and as he opened it up a shower of ten-pound notes spilled onto the bed.

'John! What's this?' I cried in amazement, wondering if I could be hallucinating from the drugs. But it was real!

John gathered up the money counting it as he went. 'There's five hundred pounds here,' he said in wonder.

'Five hundred pounds,' I gasped. 'Who's it from?'

He glanced blankly at the card and then looked inside the envelope again. There was nothing else in there. 'Well, I don't know,' he said, puzzled. 'It just says "from a friend".'

I was overwhelmed. What a kind, sweet, generous thought. Just when we'd been worrying how we were going to meet the bill. But who on earth could have done it? We spent the rest of the evening trying to guess. I wanted to thank them from the bottom of my heart.

'It must have been someone who knew you were having to pay to get this operation done,' John pointed out. But we couldn't think of anyone who was rich enough to spare five hundred pounds like that.

The weeks passed, I went home and when the bill finally arrived we were very glad of that wonderful gift. Everything was itemized separately: the fees for the room, the surgeon, the anaesthetist, the nurses, the blood. It all added up to much more than we'd thought. I had quite a few visitors during those convalescing weeks and as we talked I dropped the most outrageous hints and scoured their faces for clues – but it was no use. I was no nearer discovering the identity of my mysterious friend than I had been in hospital.

In the end I thought, this is ridiculous, I must ask the spirit world who it is so that I can thank them. I tuned in.

'I know she doesn't want me to know,' I pleaded, 'but I must show my gratitude somehow. Can't you tell me so that I can thank her?'

There was nothing for a few seconds and I thought they weren't going to tell me. Then, when I'd almost given up hope, a young woman's voice came through. It was vaguely familiar and as she spoke I remembered speaking to her some months before, during a sitting with her mother.

'It was my mum who gave you the money,' she said. 'She wanted to thank you for all you've done for her.'

Tears sprang into my eyes. This particular lady, whose name I can't mention because she says she'll be too embarrassed, was a dear, unassuming soul who had come for a sitting and remained a friend ever since. She never came to see me without bringing some little gift: a cream cake or a bottle of her daughter's favourite perfume. I should have guessed it was her – but how could she afford it? Was she going without now, because of me?

The following Monday when she came to see me I tackled her about it.

'You're very naughty, you know,' I told her as soon as she was settled with a cup of tea.

'Why? What have I done?' she asked innocently.

'You left all that money for me!' I said gently.

She blushed and stirred her tea until the bottom almost came out of the cup, but she didn't deny it.

'I really appreciate it, you know,' I went on to the top of her head, 'but it did worry me. I mean can you manage without it? It was such a lot of money?'

'Oh, yes, it's all right,' she insisted. 'I can afford it. I was left quite comfortable, you know. But how did you find out? I didn't want you to know, that's why I just put "from a friend".'

'Your daughter told me,' I explained.

'Oh,' she said. 'I never thought of that.' But she was

delighted with the explanation. It was further proof that her daughter was still with her and aware of everything she was doing.

Some months later my advance for the first book arrived but my friend wouldn't hear of being repaid. 'That money was a gift,' she insisted. 'Whatever next!'

But eventually I found a way of repaying her that I know she would approve of. On a trip to Ireland to appear on the Late Late Show, we had a few hours to spare. Our host had been reading my book and, noticing that John and I had previously worked with the mentally handicapped, he asked if we would like to visit a home for mentally handicapped children nearby. This is just the sort of thing that interests us very much and we accepted the invitation gratefully.

There followed a very happy afternoon at the Marina Clinic in Bray. The staff showed us round and we were able to talk and play with the children. I remember particularly one frail little boy with his legs in plaster who was a spastic, and we could see how nursing techniques had progressed since my nursing days. Finally, with great pride, the matron showed us a wooden trailer which was to be a treatment centre for the six stone deaf children in the home. At present they were holding coffee mornings and jumble sales to raise money for the special headphones that were needed to help teach the children to read and talk.

'We've bought one set already,' the matron told us holding them up, 'and we hope to get another five like these.'

'How much do they cost?' I asked.

'A hundred pounds each, I'm afraid,' she said. 'They're very good but they're not cheap.'

A hundred pounds each – so they needed five hundred pounds to complete the set. It was that magic figure again. I thought of my friend and the operation. She had helped me when I needed five hundred pounds, now what better way could I repay her than by helping someone else who needed the money.

'We'll buy the other five pairs,' I said quickly.

'Oh, Mrs Stokes,' gasped the matron, 'I didn't mean – I mean I wasn't . . .'

'I know,' I said, scrabbling around in my bag for my cheque book. 'But I'd like to do this for the children.' And as I bent across the desk to write out the cheque, my mind went back to the words of that old song: *'If you've had a kindness shown pass it on. It wasn't meant for you alone, pass it on.'* – and I couldn't help thinking, wouldn't it be marvellous if everyone who had received a kindness passed it on? One day my friend's kind thought will lead to five adults able to lead an almost normal life because they can read and write, and if those five adults each passed on that kindness, a chain of love could be created that might eventually stretch right round the world.

When I talk of Ramanov and his teachings, however, I must emphasise that Ramanov explains general principles only, and reminds me of them when I forget. He doesn't tell me what to do or how to solve individual problems because, as he keeps pointing out when I get exasperated, he wouldn't want to live my life for me even if he could. I'm here to learn and it's up to me to make the decisions I think best.

Some people find this very difficult to accept. The other day I had a phone call from a young woman who wanted my help. She was in constant contact with her mother in the spirit world and her mother gave her advice daily, but recently her mother had said something about a particular problem which she couldn't understand.

'I'm not sure what my mother wants me to do,' the woman explained. 'I wondered if you could find out for me.'

Whether this woman was really in touch with her mother or only believed she was, it was difficult for me to tell in a brief telephone conversation, but if what she said was true, it appalled me.

'Poor old Mum,' I said to her. 'She brought you into this world, she looked after you as a child and she probably looked after you when you married and now she's gone over you still expect her to look after you! Let your mum go. Doesn't she deserve a rest?'

'Yes, but I need her advice,' the woman insisted.

'I'm sorry, love, I can't help you,' I said. 'You're grown up now. You must work it out for yourself.'

Well, I'm afraid she didn't like that and I was sorry, but a medium's job is to act as a temporary prop to people in the depths of despair not to become a permanent crutch for the rest of their lives.

The other problem I come up against now and then is orthodox religion. Many churchmen are sympathetic but there are still a few who are very much against mediums. A few hundred years ago I would probably have been burned at the stake as a witch. A hundred years ago I might have been put in prison, but today I'm free to speak, although traditionally the church disapproves of what I do.

I came up against this problem quite recently. A lady called Barbara, distraught over the death of her seven-year-old son, came for a sitting. I have great affinity with bereaved mothers because of my own John Michael and, as often happens in cases like these, the sitting went very well. She left me in great happiness and wrote me a beautiful letter afterwards. She had got on the train to go home, crying and laughing at the same time, she wrote. Since then she had felt a great sense of relief. Part of the problem had been a tremendous feeling of guilt because, since her older son's death, she had felt locked up inside and was unable to give her younger son the affection he needed. But now the floodgates had opened and she felt warmer and more loving towards her remaining son than ever before. Even her mother had remarked on her new serenity.

I was delighted that the sitting had been of such help, so I was very surprised when Barbara phoned me a few days later in distress. Apparently she'd written excitedly to her local vicar, a friend of hers, telling him of her excitement over the sitting. She thought he would be interested. In fact he was alarmed.

'He says I should have nothing more to do with you, Doris,' Barbara sobbed. 'He said that your voices were demons who were impersonating the voices of our loved ones.'

'Yes, it does say something like that in one part of the Bible, love,' I agreed, 'I don't know why. I can only think it's to warn people not to dabble in things they don't understand. Ouija boards are very dangerous for instance; so is witchcraft and black magic and all that kind of thing. But St Paul said, "Test ye the spirits to see if they be of God" and I always do. I always offer myself in service in God's name before I start. I can't believe God would allow my work to carry on if it wasn't right.'

'But another of my friends, a Catholic, said if I came to see you again I'd be struck down dead,' Barbara sniffed.

'What a strange God she believes in to think that He would do that kind of thing to us!' I said. 'Why would He want to strike you down dead?'

'Oh, I don't know. I'm so confused, Doris,' said Barbara. 'I was brought up a Christian yet my church didn't comfort me. Oh, they tried but it didn't help. You helped me and then the vicar upset me again. I don't know what to believe.'

'Well, I fully understand, Barbara,' I told her sympathetically. 'I'll leave you to sort yourself out. I'm not pushing my ideas onto you and I don't want to make you more confused then you are already. You know where I am if you want me,' and I left it at that.

But other churchmen hold different views. When I was working at the College of Psychic Studies, I was told that a young lady was waiting to see me but wanted to know if

I would mind if she brought her vicar in with her because she was frightened.

'Yes, of course,' I said a little surprised. 'I don't mind at all.'

A nervous young woman came in and perched opposite me, followed by a pleasant open-faced clergyman. The clergyman remained quietly in the background and made no attempt to interrupt, but he glanced at his companion from time to time to see if she was all right.

I tuned in and found myself speaking to the girl's husband. He told me his name and that he'd taken his own life. I got the impression of a car parked in a beauty spot in some woods and the smell of exhaust fumes. The woman confirmed that this was correct. The man went on to talk of his children and his family.

Then another voice broke in and I knew the message was for the vicar.

'I hear the name Leonard,' I told him.

'That's my name,' he said in astonishment and I was able to give him a message from his father.

Afterwards he wrote me a beautiful letter saying that I'd done his young parishioner a world of good – in fact, two worlds: this and the next – and that he would be very grateful if I would give a talk at his church. This I later did with great pleasure and we have kept in touch ever since. In fact he still sends his parishioners along to see me when he feels I can give them more help than he can.

Theological arguments are difficult for me to follow. As far as I'm concerned the issue is a simple one. The justification for my work is the effect it has on other people. If I give lasting comfort and support then I must be doing the right thing. Every week I receive hundreds of letters of support. This is a typical example:

Dear Doris,

After a year of suffering, my mother, Ruby Lilian Hill, died of cancer. But just a minute – did I use the word die? Well, let me tell you that you have proved beyond doubt to my father and myself that there is no death, just a natural passing from the earth plane to the astral plane.

When my mother passed over my father was totally devastated. In my vain attempts to comfort him I tried to impart some of the sketchy views I had on the afterlife. But what could I, a kid (his twenty-seven-year old kid), say that could change his views on a subject he just did not believe in?

Shortly after my mother's passing I read Voices in My Ear which was serialised in a magazine. I thoroughly enjoyed the serial and felt that the honest sincerity imparted, together with the amazing accounts that you related in such easy to understand terms, would make ideal reading for a beginner in the subject. So I bought the book and suggested to my father that he read it. He was very impressed and a seed was indeed sown, but he was not altogether convinced.

However, I felt compelled to write to you, thanking you for the shred of comfort your book offered to a non-believer and after about a week you telephoned us!

My father answered the telephone and when you said, 'Hello, it's Doris Stokes,' he thought somebody was playing an unkind joke on him and he nearly replied, 'Yes, hello, I'm Tommy Cooper' which is why he probably sounded a bit unfriendly at first.

Then you said, 'I've got Ruby here' and I hadn't mentioned my mother's name in the first letter. You went on to tell us all kinds of wonderful things from my mother including that she was sorry to leave us but she'd been in such terrible pain she couldn't go on any longer. You even gave us the exact location in her body where the cancer was manifest.

The final proof came with the description of our living room. You described the layout of the furniture, the colour of the carpet and wallpaper, commented on the fact that our living room is big because we had a dividing wall knocked down making two rooms into one, you even described where the photographs are – to the right of the fireplace on a shelf!

My father was visibly moved and a great cloud seemed to have been lifted from his shoulders. People are astounded at how well he has adjusted to the loss of my mother after thirty-two years. Some *sceptics say, 'oh, well, if you believe in that — fair play to you.' But we* know, *because you Doris have proved it to us.*

With love from
Barbara Hill

When I read letters like this I know I must be doing something right. I think: you might grumble Doris, you might get tired, but if, out of ten people, you manage to prove to just one that there is life after death and a better way to live, then you're doing your job properly.

CHAPTER 13

As we walked through the gate at Dublin airport, the driver waiting to meet us clapped his hand across his eyes in mock alarm.

'Oh no,' he cried in simulated horror. 'You're the one who nearly got us shot last time!'

I couldn't help laughing. I had last visited Ireland to do a ten-minute spot on the Late Late Show and I had made very little impression on the public on that occasion. My most lasting impression had obviously been on this taxi driver – for all the wrong reasons!

He had driven us back to Dublin for our flight home only to find the airport closed because of a strike. We were diverted to Belfast in Northern Ireland.

Until then, having only visited Southern Ireland, 'the troubles', as they call them, had only been faraway scenes on the television screen but as soon as we saw the soldiers at the border check point the reality began to dawn on us.

We drove through the most beautiful, rolling, green countryside but it was littered with abandoned cars and there were too many boarded-up shops in the towns.

Belfast was a tragedy. An atmosphere of fear and hostility was clamped over the city like a lid. It was Sunday morning and people stood around their gates, but there was a sort of hush over the place. As we went on towards the Falls Road I felt sadder and sadder. Blackened, bombed-out buildings seemed to loom on every side, gaping windows stared blindly down at us, doors were boarded up and every other road appeared to have been hastily closed with old car tyres, crooked posts or police beacons.

The driver was in despair. It was some time since he had visited Belfast and so many roads were now blocked off due to bombings or shootings, we soon got hopelessly lost. We drove aimlessly around for almost half an hour before we pulled out of a side turning and found ourselves back on the main road again. In front of us was an armoured car and in the back sat a soldier with his rifle poking through the window.

Having been in the forces myself during the war, without thinking, I did what I'd always done when I saw a soldier: I raised my hand to wave.

The driver nearly had kittens. 'Oh, Holy Mary, don't move your hand! Don't move your hand!'

'I was only going to wave,' I pointed out.

'Well, you mustn't move your hand or he'll think we've got a bomb!' My insides twisted and I thought, poor Ireland, to have to live like this day after day, when you can't even wave in case they think you've got a bomb . . .

Despite my lack of impression on the Late Late Show, Gay Burn, the presenter, invited me back for another appearance in January 1981. This time I was given an hour to work with the audience and the difference it made was incredible.

The show went very well but only one communication really stands out in my mind. A boy came through who had been killed by his brother. He gave the name of his mother, who was in the audience, and the name of his brother.

The poor woman was terribly upset but she wanted me to continue, so I moved away for a few minutes to give her time to compose herself and then I went back. The young man told me there had been an argument that had got out of hand. Suddenly, a sharp pain tore through me and I knew he'd been shot or stabbed.

'Oh, my goodness!' I gasped clutching my chest.

'Yes, that's right,' sobbed the woman, knowing exactly what I meant.

It was all in a day's work to me but the effect was extraordinary. When I walked off the set, a crowd of people surged forward and pinned me to the wall in the corridor. They meant no harm, but the unexpected crush was quite alarming at first and as I struggled to smile and find out what was going on I heard a voice cry, 'Let me through! Oh, let me through! I just want to *touch* her.'

My blood went icy at her words and a strange fear prickled down my spine. What on earth did they think I was?

'Let her through, please,' I said quietly.

Two seconds later a tiny little woman emerged at the front of the crowd. She gazed up at me with a reverence that was terrifying.

'I just want to *touch* her,' she repeated as if in a daze.

'Now, look,' I said firmly. 'Don't get the wrong idea about me. I'm no one special. I'm just the same as you are. When I get back I'll have a cigarette, I'll probably have a drink and before the night's out I'll probably be swearing. Don't put me on a pedestal. I'm just the same as you.'

But it was no use. The whole place seemed to erupt. The studio was besieged by callers, the phone at the hotel didn't stop ringing and hopeful people waited for me in reception.

The morning after the show I walked into the foyer to find a group of people waiting. I had spoken to five young girls in the back row during the show and got their grandfather back for them, and now they had driven miles to come and see me with their family. I was just on my way out, but when I saw the look in their eyes I knew I would have to give them something. I tuned in and quickly found the grandfather again.

'He tells me he started an extension on the house but he didn't get it finished before he passed.'

'Yes, that's true,' they cried in delight.

'Well, he's telling me it's finished now and you're going to hang some orange curtains in it.'

'That's it,' said the father, 'and when you come to stay with us you'll sleep in the new extension!'

Another family turned up without an appointment having driven a hundred and fifty-nine miles and taken the day off work in the hope of seeing me. I had very little time but I did what I could. I got back their 'daddy', as they call their parents in Ireland.

'Your daddy says you've all clubbed together to buy a new kerb to put round his grave,' I said. 'But he's saying "I wish you'd saved your money because I'm not dead, am I?".'

He was also a little indignant with his son. 'I always said you would be late for your own funeral,' he said. 'Well, you were late for mine, and the cortège had to wait outside the gate for you.'

'Yes, that's right,' the son admitted sheepishly. 'I was held up in traffic!'

Most of my time was devoted to sittings with a few really desperate people who had booked beforehand. One of them, a small, dark-haired woman called Teresa, had lost her little boy. He was very anxious to talk to his mummy and came back straight away. He told me he was nine years old and had passed with leukaemia.

As we talked, I saw him for a split second, a thin little lad, almost bald, with just a few tufts of hair left on his head. Then he was gone, and a few minutes later he was back, but this time he had a full head of hair and was much healthier. He rushed up to his mother in his little short trousers and tried to take her hand.

'Look, Mum, look, Mum, I can run, I can jump now!' he cried, dancing round her chair to demonstrate. 'And all my hair's come back! Look!'

But of course his mother couldn't see. He disappeared again, only to return a few moments later with a red rose which he laid on her lap.

'Your little boy has just given you a red rose,' I told Teresa.

She stared sadly down at her lap which to her looked empty. 'I gave him red roses at his funeral,' she said.

'Well, he's brought you one back,' I explained.

The little boy went on to talk of his brother and his daddy who he said drove for a living and he kept mentioning a particular sweater.

'Do you mean your brother's wearing your sweater now?' I asked.

'No,' said the boy and talked of the sweater again, adding the surname, Woods.

'Well, I'm sorry, Teresa,' I said, 'I don't understand this bit. He's talking about a special sweater and the name Woods. Do you have any idea what he could mean?'

At this poor Teresa burst into tears. 'Oh, yes,' she sobbed. 'We buried him in a sweater that Mrs Woods had knitted for him.' And though she cried, Teresa was smiling through her tears, so pleased to know her son was well again and close by, even though she couldn't see him.

I was able to do another touching sitting for another bereaved mother – a woman called Mary who had lost two children tragically. They came through together, a boy called Robert and a tiny girl called Jennifer.

'It was my head, you know,' Robert, who did most of the talking, explained. 'I was bald there and it did hurt me, Mummy.'

Mary confirmed that Robert had passed with a brain tumour.

Then Jennifer talked of the little girl her parents had adopted after her death. 'My sister's got my teddy now,' she said cheerfully, not begrudging the loss of her toy at all, and Mary was thrilled to hear Jennifer acknowledge the new child as her sister.

Robert wanted to tell me about his mummy's kitchen and in a flash it formed in my mind.

'This is the oven,' said Robert, pointing it out to me, 'and here is the hob and the counter next to it and this is the breadbin and the chopping board. I come back and knock the chopping board down for Mummy to find.'

Mary's hand flew to her mouth. 'My god, they do! I'm

always finding it on the floor and wondering how on earth it got there.'

She told me afterwards that she had been to see priests and psychiatrists in an effort to get over the depression caused by the loss of her children, but only now, after the sitting, did she feel any hope for the future.

There were so many people to see that I didn't get many spare moments during the trip, but I was determined to visit the Marina Clinic in Bray before we left, to see how the children were getting on.

We drove up the rise through soft green towards the long, low building and it was as if we had never been away. Two ponies grazed in the fields, children skipped towards the car and within moments we were back in that warm, happy atmosphere, surrounded by splodgy infant paintings and battered toys. I asked after the fragile little spastic boy I'd met last time.

'Oh, I'm afraid he's not very well,' the matron told me. 'He's in bed with a cold at the moment, but you can come and see him.'

She led us to the dormitory and there he was, sitting up in bed looking at a budgie in a cage that his teacher had brought to show him.

'Now there's someone come to see you,' said the matron bustling towards him. 'You don't know who this is, do you?'

The little boy looked up and when he saw me a big grin spread across his face.

'Yes – it's Granny Doris!' he said, beaming.

I'd brought a big bag of sweets with me and I had to thrust them into his hands on the pretext of letting him choose what he wanted, while I turned to wipe away a tear. If I could have taken them all home with me I would have done.

On Sunday I was given an official day of rest and Edward, the young man who was looking after us, invited us to his home for a traditional Irish family lunch. But first he wanted to take us for a drive along the coast road because so far all we'd seen of Ireland was hotel rooms, the studios and of course the Marina Clinic.

The drive was wonderful. John and I sat with our noses pressed to the glass, unable to tear our eyes away as each mile seemed prettier than the last. We sauntered along past dark, jagged rocks, white sandy bays and a sea that shone silver grey in the weak January sun. There were castles on outcrops and tiny whitewashed cottages, and it was so warm! We'd packed our thick woollies because it was, after all, the middle of winter and very cold in London – but we didn't need them.

Finally, towards lunch-time, Edward headed back and we ended up at his modern house on a smart new estate. Within minutes the place seemed to be full of people. There was Edward's Uncle Jack, his father, Chris, and many more friends and relatives. They persuaded me to have sherry before lunch, wine with it and Irish coffee afterwards, and by the time the long, leisurely meal was over I was feeling quite merry. More and more people seemed to come and go and I couldn't keep track of them all. 'We keep open house on Sundays, Doris,' Jack explained, seeing my bemused expression.

They had had strict instructions that I was supposed to be resting and on no account were they to ask me to work, and they were very good about it. But as often happens when I'm in a very relaxed state, the voices seem to come through of their own accord.

Jack was talking to his brother-in-law, Tom, about the loss of his mammy.

'There's only one thing that really bothers me,' Jack was saying, 'and that's that there was no one with her when she died.'

Immediately I heard a voice say, 'Our Paddy was there.'

'Paddy was there,' I said without thinking.

Jack's jaw dropped. 'What did you say?'

'She says Paddy was there,' I repeated.

'By God, so he was!' cried Jack in astonishment.

Well, there was no stopping Mammy then. She talked about a family problem which she disapproved of, she said that Jack still got her handbag out from time to time, and he'd left it just the way it was when she was alive – there was even money in the purse which Anne had given her.

'Yes, that's true,' Jack admitted.

'And there's an unopened bottle of perfume still on my dressing-table,' Mammy went on. 'Give it to our Anne, I'm not going to come back to wear it.'

She was clearly very fond of Edward's father, Chris.

'He's a rash lad, our Chris,' she confided. 'But he's lovely with it. He used to drive a lorry, but not any more.'

Then she talked of the family trouble again. She sat up and folded her arms and bristled because she was very cross. I sat up in the same way to show the family what she was doing.

'Oh, God, that's your mother!' someone said to Jack because by now they had all gathered in a semi-circle round me.

'And another thing,' said Mammy, 'they've redecorated the bedroom in woodchip paper. I don't like it! I don't like it at all.'

A great gust of laughter swept round the group. 'I told you she wouldn't like it,' Chris chuckled.

After a while another voice chimed in. 'My name is Catherine Green,' she told me and her voice sounded more Scottish than Irish.

It was Edward's grandmother and it turned out she was indeed Scottish. She wanted to cuddle Edward and I leaned across and took his hand.

'She's saying this is my baby,' I told him.

'Yes, that's right. She brought me up,' Edward replied.

Catherine went on to describe her funeral which apparently had been a bit of a disaster.

'The undertaker upset the coffin and it went in wrong and so they had to take it out and do it again,' she explained. 'If they'd dug up that privet round the grave when I told them to it wouldn't have happened.'

'What do you mean, love?' I asked. 'What went wrong with the privet?'

'There were gaps in it,' she said, 'where parts of the hedge had died. One of the men slipped between the hedge and the coffin went in sideways!'

And though it was probably very traumatic at the time, the whole family fell about laughing, relieved to know that Catherine didn't mind a bit.

At the end of the impromptu sitting, Jack, who was also a wealthy businessman, reached for his wallet.

'Doris,' he said, 'I'll sign a cheque for any charity you care to name.'

'Are you sure, Jack?' I asked. 'I mean you didn't plan to have this sitting, it just happened.'

'Of course I'm sure. It was worth every penny.'

I bit my lip. Which charity should it be? There are so many I'd like to support. The Marina Clinic had already been helped so I felt someone else ought to have a turn.

'Brandon Lodge,' I said at last. 'It's an old people's home for spiritualists. They do a lot of good there and they have to rely on donations.'

So while I watched, Jack wrote out a cheque for a hundred pounds. I was thrilled. Mammy and Catherine, aided by the Irish coffee, had achieved a great deal that day.

CHAPTER 14

When I was still grieving for my son John Michael, I used to have the most marvellous dreams. Soon after I went to sleep it would seem to me that I arrived on a sunny road in the most beautiful place. There were gorgeous flowers on either side and the road sloped gently up to the brow of a hill.

At I stood there basking in the warmth of the sun, my father would appear at the top of the hill carrying my baby in his arms. He'd stride down towards me and I can still feel the indescribable joy that engulfed me as my hands touched baby skin again and I cuddled my son.

In the morning the pillow would be wet with tears but I always woke with a feeling of great happiness and serenity that lasted all day.

Just a dream, you might say, but it was a dream which recurred at regular intervals and I watched my son grow. After a while my father didn't need to carry him any more and a sturdy, apple-cheeked toddler would rush towards me, holding fast to Father's hand. I watched John Michael change over the years into a beautiful child and then a handsome young man. Until at last, when he was 16, he embraced me and told me sadly that he couldn't come to see me any more because he had to go about his Father's work.

As I learned more about spiritualism, I heard of a thing called astral travel. The theory is that while you are asleep your mind can leave your body and float around in time and space, on the astral plane, as we call it. It sounded a pretty far-fetched idea but the more I thought about it the more it seemed to fit into my special dreams. The John Michael dreams were utterly unlike any other dreams I'd had. They were as vivid and real as if they had happened.

Had I dreamed continually of my baby as a baby – the way he was when I last held him on earth – the incidents could be more easily dismissed as dreams. But the fact that I watched him change and grow up at the same rate he would have grown up on earth seemed to me to suggest that these dreams should be taken more seriously. Perhaps I had travelled on the astral plane to the spirit world.

I hadn't thought about the subject for years – after all, it's two decades now since my last dream – but reading some of the letters I received after my first book was published brought it all back. Over and over again people would write, 'Yes, it's all very well, but what is the spirit world like? That's what we want to know,' and I couldn't help thinking they had a point. Spirit contacts often do say a little about their new world but not enough for me to have built up a really detailed picture.

I turned it over in my mind, wondering how I could answer the queries and then it hit me. I would let the spirit world decide. If I really had been there all those years ago to visit my son, perhaps I could go back.

On three consecutive nights, before I went to bed, I asked silently if I could go. Nothing happened. I had my ordinary confused dreams and woke up feeling dissatisfied. Then on the fourth night, something extraordinary took place.

I was in bed asleep and yet at the same time I knew I was awake and two huge eyes were looking at me. They seemed to fill the room and they were an astonishing shade of violet. Violet eyes, I thought vaguely, John Michael had violet eyes . . . And as I watched, a face started to build up round the eyes, until I was looking at a handsome blond man and it was my son. Thirty-six years old but I would recognize him anywhere.

'John Michael!' I cried, almost bursting with pride. This beautiful creature who seemed to glow with light was my son.

'Mother, you asked if we could show you what the spirit

world is like, so I've come to take you,' he said and reached for my hand.

Suddenly we were moving. We didn't walk so much as float along effortlessly. The dark bedroom disappeared, I was bathed in bright light and without knowing how we got there, I found we had arrived at a little bungalow and I saw my parents.

'Father! Mother!' I cried, throwing my arms round them. They grinned back at me and I stared at them in amazement. They looked so well. Father looked younger, if anything, than I remembered him.

'Father looks so much younger!' I exclaimed to John Michael.

'Well, you see, Mum, those of us who come over as children grow up normally,' he explained. 'But when old people come over they lose all their aches and pains and the weariness and worry of the world. They simply feel younger and look younger because there are no infirmities, or troubles.'

I stared at my mother. There was something different about her, too, but I couldn't place it. Then I realized.

'Mum, you've got two eyes!' I said in delight. She had lost an eye at birth and I had only ever seen her with one.

'But, of course,' said John Michael, 'she's in the spirit world, isn't she? I've told you that the infirmities she had on the earth plane disappear.'

But she was still the same old Mum, bustling and ever-practical.

'That's all very well,' she said to John Michael, 'but how's she going to get back? Will she be able to go back?'

'It's okay, Gran,' John Michael smiled. 'I'll see that she gets back.'

Mum gave him a long look, then, obviously satisfied, she showed me the bungalow. 'It's all on one level, you see,' she said. 'I didn't want any stairs to clean.'

'But surely you don't have to clean?' I exclaimed. I'd

hoped that I'd leave housework behind when I passed over!

My father saw I was worried. 'No, not unless you want to,' he said. 'But you know what your mother is. Unless you can eat your meals off the lavatory floor, the house isn't clean!'

'We thought we'd show Dol the hospital, Jen,' Father went on. 'Do you want to come?'

'No, I've got far too much to do,' Mum said, starting to bustle again. 'I've got the house to finish and then I must get on with the garden.'

I smiled to myself. Typical Mum! But I was so glad she'd got her own garden at last, she had always loved plants. I hugged her again and then set off with Father and John Michael. I couldn't get over the way we floated instead of walked and, somehow, without noticing the places in between, I found we were inside the hospital.

At first glance the ward looked quite normal, with rows of beds and people standing round them. Then I noticed that the walls seemed to be made of glass looking out on to gentle rolling hills, shady trees and brilliant flowers. Everything seemed to be twice as big as on earth and I couldn't see the ceiling. I wouldn't mind being ill in a place like this, I thought. There was an extraordinary atmosphere about it. One could feel the healing in the air and it seemed to come not only from within the building, but from outside as well. Healing power seemed to wash in on invisible waves from the idyllic scenery outside the window. Instinctively, I knew that there were no operations or drugs in this hospital, the patients were cured by the atmosphere. But who were the patients?

'John Michael, why do you need hospitals over here if you lose all your infirmities when you come over?'

John Michael smiled as if he'd been waiting for me to ask that.

'Well, you see, when a person leaves his body very quickly, especially through violence or a car accident or a heart attack, they haven't had time to prepare themselves, and in that case it's a very traumatic experience for them. Imagine what it must be like to be parted from your earthly body in a split second. So they come here to recuperate, and, surrounded by their loved ones, they sleep until their spirit body recovers from the shock.'

We stood for a while watching the loving people clustered round each bed. Some of the patients were sleeping peacefully but others were sitting up, talking to their relatives, and it was clear that these people would soon be well enough to leave.

'I'm sure Mother would like to see the waiting place, Grandad,' said John Michael. Despite the fascinating scene in the hospital I was still stealing glances at John Michael. I could hardly take my eyes off him. This is my son, I had to keep reminding myself, all grown up and handsome, my son. He caught my eye and as if reading my mind, which he probably could, he put his arm round my shoulders and gave me a look of such love and tenderness I wanted to cry.

'The waiting place?' I said weakly.

'Yes, you'll see.'

We floated out of the hospital and along a little path fringed by flowers and trees. Birds swooped low over our heads and I saw a deer dart away to our right.

A few minutes later we came to a low, round building and the most exquisite woman came out to meet us. She was dressed in white, and seemed to shine, and the love that emanated from her was almost tangible. Perhaps this is where one comes to be judged, I thought, a little frightened even though I knew there was no reason to be. But they took me inside and my eyes grew in amazement. All round the walls were rows of glowing, transparent shells through which little creatures could be seen.

'But they're babies, aren't they?' I gasped. They looked just like human foetus in varying stages of growth.

'Yes, my child, they are babies,' the woman told me.

'These are the babies who didn't fulfil their full term and were sent back before they were born.'

'What happens to them?' I asked, peeping into the little silvery shells.

'They are born into the spirit world and given to spirit mothers who take care of them,' she explained.

Fascinated, I wandered round looking into each little window. Perhaps when I came over I might be given one? I felt something touch my arm.

'Come and see the nurseries, Mother,' said John Michael.

The nurseries were just behind the waiting place and they were full of laughing children. They raced, they tumbled and played boisterous games and it was hard to remember that they'd died tragically, on earth, and feel sad for them because they looked so happy. There were quite a few adults there, as well, and I was told these were either spirit mothers who brought the children up as their own, or they were relatives.

One elderly lady approached. 'Come and see my great-grandson,' she said proudly and took me to a corner where an angelic little boy was sitting on the floor playing with building bricks. When he saw me he beamed and held out his chubby little arms and I couldn't resist picking him up. I don't know what I had expected, but within seconds I was cuddling warm, solid, human flesh. There was nothing wraith-like about him.

'He came over very tragically at fourteen months old,' his great-grandmother explained. 'Fortunately I was already here so I take care of him. His name is Christopher James.'

Our tour continued. Father and John Michael wanted to show me as much as possible in a short time. We visited a school where lessons were given in thought only, and then we went on to a hall of music where one could choose what one wanted to listen to from the variety of pieces coming from the different areas of the building.

We came upon a little room where a young man was playing the organ, totally absorbed in the music he was making. From nowhere I picked up a thought like a voice, 'He couldn't play a thing on the earth plane but this was always inside him, and here he can express it.'

'Isn't that remarkable,' I said to Father and John Michael, 'I've always wanted to make music.'

'When you come over, Mother, you will have the chance to express yourself,' John Michael said, 'and if you want to learn to make music you shall.'

From there we went on to the vast Hall of Learning. I was totally overwhelmed. The walls and pillars shone with colour: rose, mauves and blues swirled into each other over the creamy stone as if it was alive. I thought it would be warm, but when I slid my fingers over the smooth surface, I found it was cool.

Thousands and thousands of people were gathered in the hall. Some sat with their arms folded and legs crossed like buddhists, some slumped comfortably and others lay back with their eyes closed, and yet I knew that they were listening to the teacher with complete attention.

I blinked as my eyes came to rest on the teacher. One moment he appeared very very old, thousands of years old, it seemed, and yet when I looked again he was a young man.

He was communicating to the students in thought. I wonder if I could ask him a question? I thought idly, without realizing what I was doing.

The teacher looked up instantly and turned to me. 'Greetings, my child!'

I jumped, startled. I hadn't said a word. Clearly he had picked up my thoughts.

'I would like to ask you a question,' I said nervously. He nodded encouragingly. 'Well, can you tell me what is happening on our earth plane? We seem to be in a terrible mess.'

'I know, my child,' he said. 'God gave you a beautiful

world to live in and you are destroying it by man's inhumanity to man. Until you learn to love one another, then you will continue to destroy the world.'

I must confess I was disappointed. Well, I know *that*, I thought, forgetting that the thought wasn't private, that's just common sense.

'Don't jump to conclusions, my child. Wait until I've finished,' he said gently. 'There comes a time when, if you violate God's law, then you each have to pay for it. Unfortunately, many innocent people, babies and children, get caught, too. Learn to love one another more, feel the love that is in this place. I tell you, child, when these souls came here they were each enveloped in their own individual religion, were each wrapped up in their own material condition, and yet look at them now. Feel the love.' And at this all the students turned to each other and although no words were spoken one could feel the love reaching out one to the other.

'This is what we try to teach you on the earth plane,' the teacher continued, 'but you just won't listen.'

I suppose I was a bit stung by this. 'Well, I try very hard,' I said, a little indignantly.

He smiled. 'We're all human. We've all trodden this path. We know how difficult it is, but think of it as if you had a light within you, that God has given to every one of us that divine light. It's only a small light within you and it's only a small light within the other people you meet, so therefore one light cannot do much good on its own. But, child, if all those lights were joined together, then it would light up the darkness. That is what you have to try to do.

'Do not say in your work, "we have the right way". None of us has the right way. We all have something to learn from each other.'

Then he pointed to the farthest corner of the hall and for the first time I noticed there was a man standing there. He was quite free to move and yet I could sense an invisible barrier around him as if he was in a cage.

'He desperately wants to join us,' said the teacher, 'but he's still hidebound in his own religion, which he thinks is the only way. He hasn't yet learned how to let down the barrier and say, "I am just one of God's children". But he comes every day and soon the barriers will dissolve and he will feel the love.' As he pointed, all the people turned round and sent their love across to the man. At once his face started to brighten with a smile and he took one step forward, then stopped uncertainly.

'Now that is good,' said the teacher. 'He has taken one step. That is enough. He will come in his own time. You must understand that over here no one is pressured, we just give them our love, teach them what we know and what we've learned and they come to us in their own time when they feel their soul is open.

'I have to talk to you as an earthling. Your soul needs the tears. Think of a flower; it cannot bloom and it cannot survive without rain. It cannot blossom out into its full beauty without the sun. So think, if you can, of that divine part of you in your earthly body and when you have tragedy and tears, think of them as the rain falling to feed it, and then when the joyous times come, when something beautiful happens and your heart is full of joy, then that is the sun that is nurturing that fragile flower.'

'What happens if someone who has been very bad comes over at the same time as somebody who has tried to live their life on a spiritual level?' I asked.

'You are as you are,' said the teacher. 'Two people can come over at the exact same second and one will see the most beautiful flowers and blue lakes and mountains with snow peaks. The other soul, who has gone through life treading on everybody because he was determined to get what he wanted out of life and didn't care who he hurt to get it, will see dark forbidding water and trees without leaves. Like attracts like.'

This sounded too much like the old-fashioned ideas of Hell to me.

'Well, where do they go?' I asked John Michael.

'The path of progression is open to every soul,' he said. 'God doesn't close his doors on anyone, but they have to start at the bottom.'

'Do you think it would be possible to see it?' I asked.

'Do you really want to go, Mother? You might feel very unhappy. We feel unhappy. But until these people can put out their hands to their guides who are there, who give up their lives to help them, they can't start on the upward path.'

For a split second he showed me this place and it was dreadful. It was cold and grey and there was a bitterness and ill feeling that could be tasted. I shuddered, and in a flash I was back again.

'We don't like it either, Mother,' said John Michael, seeing my stricken face. 'But don't worry. They don't stay there. They are never left alone and sooner or later the love gets through to them and they start to climb upwards.'

Just before we left, John Michael pointed out two girls and a boy.

'These are my sisters and my brother,' he said.

And before I could answer, one of the girls, a pretty lass with brown hair, came over and kissed me. 'Hello, Mother,' she said.

I didn't know what to say to her. These must be the three babies I lost before birth but I felt helpless with guilt. They were just strangers to me. I couldn't love them the way I loved John Michael.

When she had gone, I turned to my father in distress. 'I can't love her, Dad,' I said.

'Look, Dol, you didn't know these babies,' Father pointed out, 'so there's no need to worry. The love link is eternal and when you come over the love will be there.

'But for now, the only thought in your head should be your job. We're very proud of you. You're doing your work well, so keep on doing it and we'll do all we can to help you from this side.'

I started to cry because I knew the end of my visit was near and I couldn't bear to leave these two men I loved so much.

John Michael put his arms round me. 'It's time to go back, Mother,' he said. 'I'm busy and so are you. Keep doing your work, Mum, and I'll keep doing mine.'

The the scene dissolved and I remember no more until I woke up the next morning in my own bed, with tears streaming down my face.

So was it a dream? It was so clear and real and detailed that I can't believe it was only a dream. It is fresh and vivid to me now as it was the morning I woke up. It felt like a real experience. So, people can call me a crank if they like, but as far as I'm concerned I've been to the spirit world, I've seen what it's like and I can say, quite truthfully, that it's beautiful.

All Futura Books are available at your bookshop or newsagent, or can be ordered from the following address:
Futura Books, Cash Sales Department,
P.O. Box 11, Falmouth, Cornwall.

Please send cheque or postal order (no currency), and allow 45p for postage and packing for the first book plus 20p for the second book and 14p for each additional book ordered up to a maximum charge of £1.63 in U.K.

Customers in Eire and B.F.P.O. please allow 45p for the first book, 20p for the second book plus 14p per copy for the next 7 books, thereafter 8p per book.

Overseas customers please allow 75p for postage and packing for the first book and 21p per copy for each additional book.